International Trade Operations

YOKOYAMA Kenji

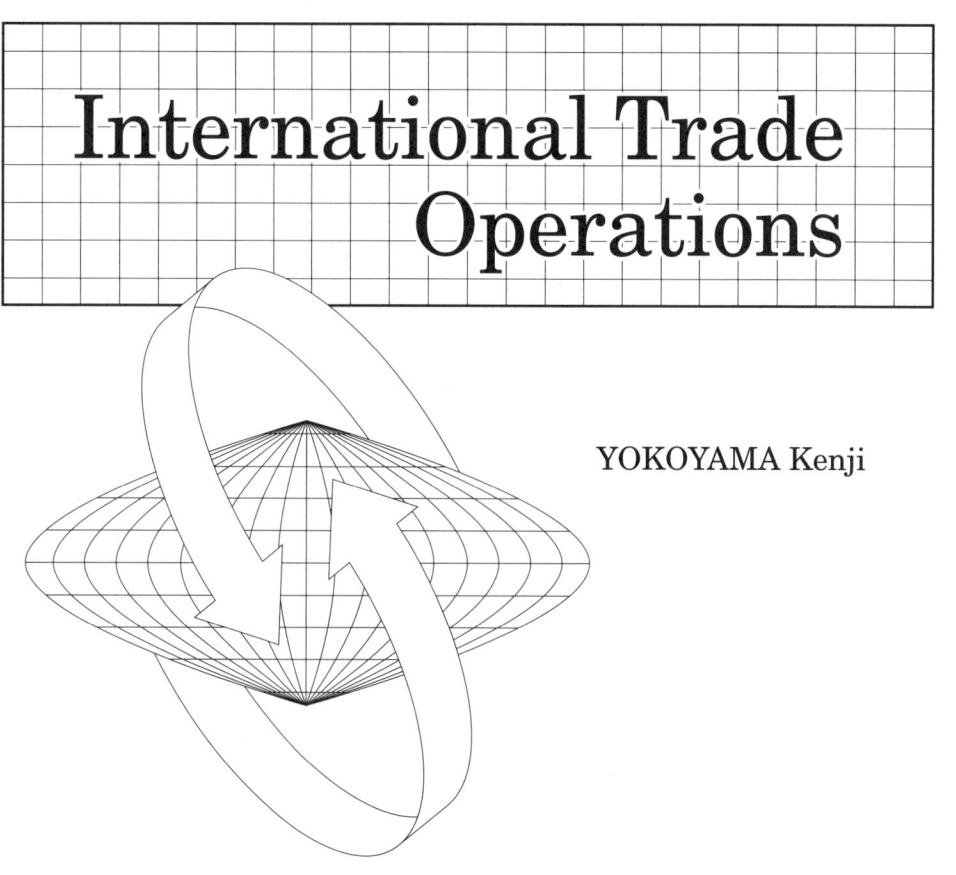

UNIVERSITY EDUCATION PRESS

Yokoyama Kenji, Ph.D. Professor
Graduate School of Management
Ritsumeikan Asia Pacific University (APU)

Preliminary translated by:
Jiang Yong Li, College of Asia Pacific Management, APU
Megarini Puspasiri, College of Asia Pacific Management, APU
Melody Nelson, College of Asia Pacific Studies, APU
Nguyen Thi Ngoc Lan, Graduate School of Management, APU
Noimarkyar Nareerad, College of Asia Pacific Management, APU
Wang Sandy, Fujitsu Corporation
Zhang Fei, College of Asia Pacific Management, APU

Published in 2006
By University Education Press
Okayama, Japan

© Yokoyama Kenji, 2006

All Rights Reserved
Printed in Japan

Preface

This book is an introduction to international trade operations. There are three reasons why I encouraged myself to write it.

Firstly, although trade operations is a traditional field in Japan's advanced commercial education, the textbooks available are either too detailed that they can only be used as dictionaries or they only contain a list of facts. There are few appropriate textbooks for this study.

Trade operations consist of many detailed facts that can be written easily. From that alone, however, philosophies and worldviews cannot be perceived and understood by beginners.

However, you cannot explain the bases of trade operations only by illustrations or cartoons alone. As an independent scholarship system, trade operations have its own world and all its items and facts are related organically. Beginners will not grasp the idea if the relationships among all the factors are not explained properly.

Secondly, universities with a semester system are increasing. Courses that used to consist of 24 - 25 lectures are now 12 - 14 lectures. Old textbooks written for a full-year's course may be too long and detailed for one semester and the relations among the factors cannot be explained clearly. As a consequence, students may fail to catch the whole image and complain about its difficulty.

The last reason is that trade practice is shifting from specialized education to generalized education. Until recently, trade operations have been a subject for training specialists. Today, trade operations education for specialists is declining and on the contrary, generalized education is badly needed. For example, the position of trade operations in university education is under management rather than commerce. Its objective is to build one's management skills in which an individual transaction can be evaluated, thus is different from the objective of specialized education.

For these reasons, this textbook can be defined as an

"introductory book for management education under a semester system."

I mentioned, "encouraging myself" earlier because writing an introduction book is always difficult regardless of the field. In order to explain the basic items precisely whilst properly disregarding any unnecessary items, it is necessary to perceive every single factor and capture the philosophy of the whole image. In this sense, I needed to encourage myself to write it.

The book would not have been published without the patience and advice from Mr. SATO Mamoru of University Education Press, who was patient until I finished the manuscript. I sincerely express my thanks to him.

RITSUMEIKAN APU   YOKOYAMA Kenji

May 9, 2006

International Trade Operations
Contents

Preface

Introduction   Understanding International Trade Operations   1
Summary
1   What Is Trade Operations   1
2   Related Organizations of Trade Transaction   4
3   Three Steps of Trade Transaction   7
Questions   12

Part 1   Contract Conclusion

Chapter 1   Finding Transaction Partners and General Terms and Conditions   14
Summary
1   International Marketing   14
2   Determining Transaction Partner   16
3   Credit Inquiry   18
    3-1   Necessity of Credit Inquiry
    3-2   Contents of Credit Inquiry
    3-3   Access of Credit Inquiry
4   Engagement on General Terms and Conditions   20
    4-1   Necessity of General Term and Conditions
    4-2   Agency and Distributorship Agreements
    4-3   Content of General Terms and Conditions
    4-4   Discord over Contract
Questions   30

Chapter 2   Price Quotation and Trade Terms   31
Summary
1   Negotiation of Quality and Price   31
    1-1   Ways for Determining Quality and Price
    1-2   Price List

		1-3	Price Quotation	
2	Trade Terms			36
		2-1	The Function of Trade Terms	
		2-2	International Unification Rules of Trade Term	
		2-3	Conditions of Incoterms	
		2-4	Terms Used in Practice	
Questions				46

Chapter 3   Specific Terms and Conditions   47
Summary
1   Formation of Sale Contract   47
    1-1   Negotiation Process
    1-2   Offer and Order
    1-3   Drafting Contract
2   Content of Specific Terms and Conditions   51
    2-1   Quality
    2-2   Quantity
    2-3   Price
    2-4   Payment
    2-5   Cargo Insurance
    2-6   Delivery
Questions   61

Part 2   Contract Fulfillment Preparation

Chapter 1   Obtaining License of Export and Import   64
Summary
1   Export and Import License   64
    1-1   Trade Control Institution
    1-2   Export License
    1-3   Obtaining Export License
    1-4   Obtaining Import License

| 2 | Obtaining Other Certificates | 70 |
| Questions | | 71 |

Chapter 2 Logistics Arrangement 73
Summary
1	Requesting Forwarders	73
2	Types of international Transport	75
3	Marine Transport	80
	3-1 Sea Fare	
	3-2 Liner Contract	
	3-3 Charter Contract	
	3-4 Bill of Landing and Sea Waybill	
4	Air Transport	89
	4-1 Air freight	
	4-2 Air Transport Contract and Air Waybill	
5	Combined Transport	92
	5-1 Combined Transport Fare	
	5-2 Combined Transport Contract and Documents	
Questions		94

Chapter 3 Insurance Arrangement 95
Summary
1	Cargo Insurance	95
	1-1 Necessity of Cargo Insurance	
	1-2 Terminology of Cargo Insurance	
	1-3 Insurance Policy	
	1-4 Insurance Conditions	
	1-5 Insurance Period	
	1-6 Conditions of New Insurance Policy	
	1-7 Cargo Insurance Contract	
	1-8 Insurance Documents	
	1-9 Air Cargo insurance	

				Contents vii

  2   Trade Insurance   105
        2-1   Function of Trade Insurance
        2-2   Types of Trade Insurance
  3   Product Liability Insurance   107
        3-1   What Is Product Liability
        3-2   Details of Product Liability Insurance
Questions   109

Chapter 4   Payment and Trade Finance Arrangement   111
Summary
1   Letter of Credit (L/C)   111
        1-1   What is L/C
        1-2   Insurance of L/C
        1-3   Types of L/C
        1-4   Trade Contract of L/C
        1-5   Contents of L/C
2   Drawing bill of Exchange   122
3   Trade Finance
        3-1   Method of Avoiding Insolvency Risk   125
        3-2   Trade Finance
4   Avoiding Foreign Exchange Risk   127
        4-1   Foreign Exchange Risk
        4-2   Avoiding Foreign Exchange Risk
Questions   132

Part 3   Contract Fulfillment

Chapter 1   Export Customs Entry and Shipping   134
Summary
1   Export Customs Entry Procedure   134
        1-1   Preparation before Transport
        1-2   Bonded Area Entry and Measurement

viii

		1-3	Export customs entry	
2	Shipping Procedure			138
		2-1	Marine Transport	
		2-2	Air Transport	
3	Shipping advice			140
Questions				141

Chapter 2　　Trade Payment　　　　　　　　　　　　143
Summary
1　Preparation of Documentary Bill of Exchange (Draft)　　143
2　How to Read the List of Exchange Rates　　　　　　　146
3　Open Account Payment　　　　　　　　　　　　　　147
4　Payment by Documentary L/C　　　　　　　　　　　148
　　　4-1　Export Payment
　　　4-2　import Payment
5　Payment by Documentary Bill of Exchange Collection　151
6　Guarantee Delivery　　　　　　　　　　　　　　　　153
Questions　　　　　　　　　　　　　　　　　　　　　153

Chapter 3　　Import Customs Entry and Cargo Receiving　155
Summary
1　Import Customs Entry and Tariff System　　　　　　　155
　　　1-1　Import customs entry Procedure
　　　1-2　Tariff System of Japan
2　Import Cargo Receiving　　　　　　　　　　　　　　157
　　　2-1　Transport Means and Cargo Receiving Preparation
　　　2-2　Liner Cargo Receiving
　　　2-3　Charter Cargo Receiving
　　　2-4　Air Cargo Receiving
3　Insurance Claim　　　　　　　　　　　　　　　　　　160
　　　3-1　Discovering Damage and Procedure Afterwards
　　　3-2　Claim to Exporter and Shipping Company

	3-3	Claim to Insurance Company	
4	Trade Claim		164
	4-1	What Is Trade Claim	
	4-2	Claim Bring and Problem Settlement	
	4-3	Arbitration and Lawsuit	
	4-4	Claim Handling Procedure	
Questions			167

Main References   168

Index   170

Introduction
Understanding Trade operations

Summary

Trade operations will be explained in this chapter. This chapter is a summary of what is written in this book. An explanation will be made on how organizations are related to trade transaction functions. Finally, the process of trade transaction will be introduced. Here, the process will be separated into three stages: contract conclusion stage, contract fulfillment preparation stage and contract fulfillment stage.

1 What Are Trade Operations?

What is trade? Although trade cannot be easily defined, it is related to the selling of goods and its movement from one country to another. The goods can be called "item" which refers to all visible and tangible things. Thus, trade means the "movement of items that crosses the borders".

Not only do items move but production technology can also be transacted. Sometimes, the right to use a certain character is transacted and moved as well. Such invisible things are called "service". Service transaction has become active due to economic development and the rising importance of information. Therefore, this service transaction should also be included in the definition. Trade can be defined as "movement of items and service that crosses national borders".

Trade refers to the transaction and movement of items and services among several countries. However, the term trade in the sentence, "Japan's post-war economy had been supported by trade" is quite different from that of, "My grandfather earned money by trade".

The previous usage refers to trade involving the whole of Japan while the latter one refers to a concrete trade transaction. This can also be called the macro aspect and micro aspect of trade. The definition "movement of items and service that crosses borders" can be understood in two different perspectives; from the perspective of the entire country and the perspective of an individual trade transaction.

Two methods can be used to observe trade. One of which is to observe from the perspective of the whole country or the whole world, and the other one is to observe from the perspective of each single concrete transaction. From a macro perspective, the object of research can be trade features in a country or a region, the relationship between domestic economy and trade or foreign exchange, the government's trade policy, and so on. If trade transaction is observed on the level of an individual transaction, there are fields called trade operations, trade commerce or trade transaction theory.

Trade is the "movement of items and service that crosses national borders". Because of that, more difficulties are involved compared to domestic transaction; for example, the problems of communication gap and intercultural understanding. No matter how sincere the transaction participants are, unexpected problems will occur if the ideologies are different. Climate and geographical conditions are risk factors as well. Even the distance for transportation would increase the possibility of goods being damage. From these points, conducting business safely is the first issue in the research of trade operations. Throughout the history of world trade industry, institutions and customs for avoiding risks have been formed. How to practice trade safely is an important objective for trade operations studies.

"A safe transaction" is one important part of the definition of trade operations. However, since people do the trade operations as a form of economy activity, gaining profits are also an important issue. This "economic rationality" is one aspect of trade.

Generally, if risks are to be avoided during transaction, some costs will be involved. On the contrary, if profit is prioritized, risks are inevitable. A secure transaction and a transaction prioritizing profits are not compatible; instead there is a discrepancy between the two. In business, balance is taken in such conflicting problems. Therefore, not only security but rationality is also necessary when defining trade operations. Yet, it cannot be said that these two aspects are explained well in the research field of trade operations. Nowadays, economical rationality is well interpreted through concepts of the marketing field and logistics field. "Trade operations", which will be explained here, will be focused mainly on how to avoid risks. In summary, trade operations can be defined as "a research field for secure and rational individual trade".

Here, let's take a closer look at "individual trade". In trade transaction, the object of goods and service moves. As it is difficult to define the movement of service, it will not be considered as an object of trade in the book. Only the movement of goods will be explained here. Goods moved from one country to another by trade will be discussed. This is also called physical distribution or abbreviated as distribution.

The seller, as an exporter, signs a contract with the buyer, the importer. While the goods move from the seller to the buyer, the possessive right also moves at a certain time. Such movements of possessive rights are called commercial distribution or abbreviated as commerce.

In the process of individual trade, two movements of physical distribution and commercial distribution are involved. Yet, these are not the only processes. The movement of cash also exists when the buyer pays the seller; this is called "finance". Thus, in individual trade, distribution, commerce and finance are involved.

Therefore, trade operations can be defined as "research on the institutions, customs and procedures for safe and rational individual trade" which is composed of distribution, commerce and finance.

2 Related Organizations of Trade Transaction

The players in a trade transaction are the exporter (seller) and the importer (buyer). There are exporters who export products made by their own firms and there are those who export products bought from domestic dealers. A business firm belongs to the latter category. In the case of import, there are manufacturers who import for their own use and there are also business firms who import in order to resale.

If the manufacturer has a lack of knowledge in the area of international business, it will ask a trade firm to undertake the export procedure. Even in this occasion, the exporter is the manufacturer since the business firm exports only in the name of the manufacturer.

The exporters sometimes name an agency or distributor as the dealer of the import place and carries out sales activity there. Both agents and distributors transfer the management rights of the exporter's products to the importers. However, the agency only searches for buyers for the exporters, then signs a contract in place of the exporters; they cannot buy the products in their own name. Agencies ask the exporters to pay a certain proportion of the transaction fee as a "commission." Yet, distributors buy the products and resell them to make the margins. Dealers who do such transactions, bear the risks and hold themselves responsible are referred to as "principal". Distributors are principals in this sense.

On the contrary, there are cases when the importers appoint the exporters their agents and ask for a purchase. Such dealers are called "buying agents."

Most big business firms and manufacturers possess local offices and local corporate bodies in the main countries. In this case, trade transaction is done by the main office and branches. Such transactions are called "inter-office transaction."

In this book, transactions between exporters and importers who have no relation as agencies and distributors, nor the main office and branches, are referred to as inter-independent-firm transaction.

Trade transaction realizes the flow of goods and cash between exporters and importers; this cannot be realized solely by exporters and importers. As shown in Figure 1, many related organizations allow for goods and cashed to be moved smoothly. The relation of other organizations is explained in Figure 1.

Firstly, let's examine the government. The government manages trade transactions in various aspects. There are export and import of cargo that can influence the security of a country or even the world. There are restrictions that need to be made when considering environmental protection. Also, some restrictions are necessary to protect domestic industries. Under such conditions, the government enforces importers and exporters to be licensed. When cargo is transferred from export and import, tariff must be paid at the Customs clearance. In Japan, the Ministry of Economy and Industry is in control over the acquisition of licenses; Customs comes under the Ministry of Finance. Also, a part of the cargo is managed by the Ministry of Welfare and Labor. Therefore, the term of government here refers to all government-related organizations that control trade in some way.

Compared to domestic transactions, trade transaction involves far more risks of a larger scale. The first risk is cargo damage and loss when transporting. This risk increases with the distance of transportation. Cargo damage during transportation is guaranteed by the cargo insurance of insurance companies. Insurance companies are also the insurers of product liability insurance. Product liability means that the manufacturer takes responsibility if the consumers receive damage when using the products. Product liability insurance is an insurance institution that is built for covering the manufacturers' damage compensation. An insurance institution also exists for the trade contract itself. This is called trade insurance. This insurance covers the loss when the cargo cannot be exported, even though the contracted is signed, due to the importers' bankruptcy, strikes or wars. In Japan, the insurer of the trade insurance is not an insurance company, but the Japan Trade Insurance, an independent administrational corporate body.

Trade cargo is carried from the export place to the import place by international transportation means of ship or aircraft. In the case of Japan, a combination of transportation by ship and land or ship and aircraft is practiced, in addition to the two transport means. The dealers that possess such international transportation means are called international carriers and they are referred to as shipping companies and airline companies.

Figure 1   Related organizations of trade transaction

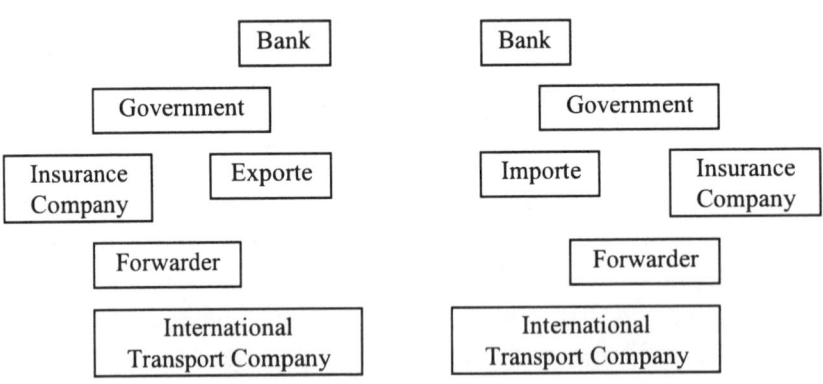

Exporters and importers make agencies sign cargo insurance contracts and international transportation contracts rather than signing them by themselves. Such dealers generally possess domestic transport means such as trucks and play the role of Customs dealers. Moreover, they efficiently carry out the procedure from loading to clearance and shipping at the export place, or from import clearance to cargo transaction and finally to warehouse stocking. Such dealers are called forwarders. Forwarders and international carriers carry out the distribution of trade transactions.

Banks also play an important role. Trade transaction is composed of distribution, commerce and finance. Banks carry out the financial procedures. Banks realize the flow of cash. Most trade payments are carried out through banks. Sometimes, banks outside the export and import places are also involved. In the actual flow of cash, banks also provide other financial services. Among these services, there are export and import loans, future exchange reservation for avoiding foreign exchange risks, option transaction, and so on. Such financial services related with payment are called trade finance.

3 Three Steps of Trade Transaction

Trade transaction is done among countries and areas with different languages, customs, culture, climate, and so on. As a result, unexpected incidents occur far more then when compared with that of domestic transaction. Throughout history, people have attempted to resolve such problems through customs, institutions and procedures. Trade practice explores the aggregation of such customs, institutions and procedures.

With the development of trade, trade operations have become more complicated. Students who are studying trade operations and the people involved in this business often say, "Trade practice is difficult" or "I'm only doing my business; it is difficult to understand the relation with other practices". It is difficult to understand the whole picture because focus is placed on each single practice. In the study of trade operations, each single practice should be learnt. At the same time, the position of each single practice within the whole system should be understood.

Those who will study trade operations should try to capture the bigger picture of trade transaction. Trade operations are easily understood when considering the three stages of "contract conclusion", "contract fulfillment preparation" and "contract fulfillment".

In the stage of contract conclusion, the exporter and importer gather to negotiate about the transaction, reach an agreement and conclude a business contract. Concretely speaking, the object of study is general terms and conditions, trade terms for price quotation and individual conditions.

An inter-independent-firm business contract is generally composed of general terms and conditions and specific terms and conditions. Items that are related to the overall contract are made before the individual contracts. This is general term and condition. Based on that, contracts are made for each single business transaction. This is called an individual contract.

In trade transaction, Trade Terms are used as a basis for price calculation. There are presented by abbreviations such as FOB and CIF and are written behind the price. They are important conditions that must be used when estimating prices or determining prices by contracts. Students of trade operations must remember these trade transaction terminologies.

Contracts are not executed soon after conclusion as preparation is necessary. As this preparation is extremely complicated, we will understand it through each trade related institute.

First of all, the government's practice is trade license application. However, there are some cases when the export or import license should be applied for beforehand.

In the case of export, when the import country asks, the pre-shipping examination, quarantine certification and origin place certification should be acquired. Though inspection organizations and certification organizations are not always government related, here we will consider them as part of the governmental procedure. Moreover, when importing agriculture products or mining industry products from developing countries, application on special tariff (low tariff), if it is to be used, should be made beforehand in the Customs.

Next is the transportation arrangement. In this book, this

procedure is replaced by the expression "logistics arrangement". A dealer called a forwarder is depended on in both export and import. As most forwarders play the role of domestic carriers, Customs clearance dealers, insurance agencies, shipping companies and agents of airline companies, the whole procedure from the arrangement of domestic and international transport to that of clearance and insurance can be completed at once.

In the arrangement of international transport, either sea transport, air transport or compound transport is chosen. The trade terms determine whether the exporters or importers arrange the transportation. Importers arrange according to FOB while exporters arrange according to C&F and CIF. In the case of FOB, sometimes the exporters make arrangements instead of the importers. In the case of most air cargo and small lots of marine cargo, the transport contract is directly signed with the shippers' agency of forwarders.

The next practice concerns insurance. Trade terms determine when fee liability transfers from the exporters to the importers. However, when CIF trade terms are used, the exporters must arrange the cargo insurance for the importers according to the business contract. With other trade terms, the exporters and importers insure their own cargo. Moreover, instead of applying to the insurance companies directly for cargo insurance, exporters and importers are more likely to sign contracts through forwarders who are also agencies for insurance companies. If necessary, product liability insurance and trade insurance should also be concluded at this stage.

Next is the practice towards banks. In this book, the expression "arrangement of payment and trade finance" is used. When an agreement is reached by using the letter of credit as a payment assurance in the contract, the importer requires the transaction bank to make a letter of credit. This letter of credit is delivered to the exporter through the bank in the export place. Upon receiving it, the exporter should examine carefully whether there is a problem in the letter of credit.

There is a foreign exchange fluctuation risk in transactions involving foreign currencies. For example, when the price is shown in Euro or Dollar from Japan's perspective, it is possible that the Yen received is actually higher or lower then expected since the exchange rate fluctuates. If the amount is higher, there is no problem. However, if the amount is lower, measures should be taken beforehand to avoid the risk. In general, future exchange is reserved to the banks, which determines the exchange rate of Yen and foreign currencies.

If necessary, exporters and importers apply for a loan at the banks. There are various kinds of loans for trade transaction. They will be easy to use if the contract is signed.

The third stage of trade transaction is "contract fulfillment". This means the actual movement of goods and cash. This also means that while it is obligatory for exporters to hand over the cargo to the importers, the importers are obligated to pay money to the exporters. Although this stage of "fulfillment preparation" can also be regarded as a part of "fulfillment" in some aspects, here fulfillment stage only refers to the stage of real movement.

The "contract fulfillment" stage can be divided into four concrete stages. In the first stage, cargo is moved out of the warehouse, carried to an export harbor, and loaded after the export customs entry. In the second stage, the exporter requires the banks to make the payment and in the third stage, the importer executes the payment through the banks. In the fourth stage, the importer receives cargo from the import harbor after the cargo's import Customs entry.

Domestic transport, Customs entry and shipment inside export place; import Customs entry, cargo receiving and domestic transport inside the import place are not done by the exporters and importers themselves but by the forwarders who play the roles of the domestic carriers, the Customs clearance dealers, and marine cargo dealers. Exporters transfer documents that are necessary for shipment and clearance such as shipment plan and commercial invoice, to the forwarders and entrust all the operations. Similarly, the importers transfer documents that are necessary for the Customs clearance and for receiving cargo from shipping companies or airline companies, to the forwarders and entrust all the operations.

After receiving the cargo, if some cargo happens to be damaged or the contracted cargo is missing, the importer will ask the shipping companies for claim proceedings, ask for insurance from the insurance companies, or directly make a claim to the exporters.

The major procedure of trade transaction has been explained above. The practices are rarely done in a sequence from contract conclusion to contract fulfillment preparation to contract fulfillment. There are cases when the cargo must be shipped although the contract is not signed. Such cases often occur when cargo shipment preparation is done while the exporter has not received the letter of credit yet.

It is important to know what occurs in each stage. In other words, the relations of the particular practice and other practices, and its position in the whole procedure must be always clear. This is because most problems are caused due to the relations of each practice. One should consider how one practice can influence another. Moreover, predicting beforehand is the best way to prevent problems.

This book is written in order of the three stages, "contract conclusion", "contract fulfillment preparation" and "contract fulfillment". It is required that the learners keep in mind the position of each single practice in relation to the entire system.

Questions

1 Name the related organizations of trade transaction and explain their roles.
2 Explain the procedure of trade transaction by dividing it into three stages.
3 Discuss the meaning of the expression "trade transaction is the aggregation of customs and institutions" and prepare in class.

Part 1 Contract Conclusion

Chapter 1
Specifying Transaction Partners and General Terms and Conditions

Summary

The procedure from finding transaction partners to concluding general terms and conditions will be explained in four parts of international marketing: looking for a transaction partner, credit research and general terms and conditions contents. It is important that students understand the necessity and contents of the general terms and conditions. In addition, the meaning of agency contract and distributorship agreement should be well grasped.

1 International Marketing

While we are moving deeper into the concrete contents of trade, learners are required to have minimum knowledge about international marketing since it has a direct impact on international trade. For example, in marketing research, when assigning an agency to do transaction instead of an independent firm, the procedure for finding partners and the contents of a contract differ. In this way, international marketing deeply affects trade operations.

Since we mainly focus on international trade, only the fundamental contents of international marketing will be explained here, which will enable students to understand international trade.

What indeed is international marketing? The image of international marketing can be grasped if there are some ideas of what is the object of study in marketing. Commodity is distributed and sold through the market. Marketing is a scientific study and analysis of how such a commodity is rationally distributed and sold. When this distribution occurs internationally, it is called international marketing. Export is often regarded as representing the entire concept of international marketing but, here, import transaction is also considered a part of it.

One important point of international marketing is to obtain general information of the transaction partner's market. For example, in the case of import into Japan, not only the exporter but the importer should also get general information about Japan. Domestic information can be easily neglected. General information refers to information about the export partners' country such as climate, geography, religion, government policy, and social system. When exporting, a company has to research many different countries in order to find the best and suitable market.

Law and regulations such as commerce laws and economical laws should be especially studied. For example, when appointing a sales agency, it is necessary to research whether or not there are laws protecting the agencies in the import country. Moreover, it is important to pay attention to domestic laws which may have regulations for different categories of import cargo.

After acquiring such general information, more concrete contents should be investigated and researched in order to determine necessary issues. Such research and decisions are made on specific products about transaction items, sales route, price and promotion.

For transaction products, decisions should be made on how the design will match the export market, or the domestic market when importing, and what the package should be.

For the sales route, a decision should be made on whether to use inter-independent-firm transaction, or to specify an agency and distributor to do a transaction, or to do a transaction after setting up the branch, office or local corporation body. In the case of import, a decision should be made on whether to import by setting a buying agency or not and how to deal with the domestic sales route. Moreover, it should be determined whether to entrust business firms or not with the export and import practices.

Next, the product price should be determined. In export, the price is the sales price; in the case of import, it refers to the purchase limit price which depends on the domestic market conditions. There are two methods to calculate the product price. One is to add on the actual cost which is called the cost plus method. The other one is to determine the expected price range and operate the cost inside the range. This is called the break down method. Concrete ideas of price quotation will be explained in Chapter 2.

For sales promotion, effective advertisement measures and sales promotion measures should be determined. Promotion will be made overseas for export and domestically for import.

International marketing practice is making a decision based on the research of an individual content after obtaining general information.

2 Determining Transaction Partner

In international marketing, after dealing with the product, price and the distribution channel, sales promotion and the target market, traders usually search for business partners (exporter for importer and importer for exporter) and then start the negotiation process. Though there are cases when the transaction proceeds after the partner is found, there are also several other ways for finding new partners.

First of all, there are many organizations that are developing international business matching such as Chambers of Commerce, Trading Associations, and JETRO/ Japan External Trade Organization. Since various dealers send e-mail and letters as application files to these organizations, traders can easily find an appropriate partner. Traders can also send transaction application forms to the organizations in the target market. Moreover, there is a trade negotiation institute that keeps a directory of businesspersons. Traders can select anyone from the list to be their partner.

In recent years, there are a number of websites that help business partners match up. Some will take a commission fee but others provide free service. JETEO is one which provides free service for traders. Upon registration, information will be sent to the related dealers automatically.

Moreover, international trade fairs are another good source where traders can find partners since their products will be displayed. Various categories such as countries and industries are featured at this fair. Even when suitable partners are not found, international trade fairs are worth attending since traders can find out about new market trends and be recognized themselves. Another option for exporters is using magazines that are published in the target market to publicize their goals. Despite the cost of advertisement, it can be very efficient and successful if the advertisements attract a great many traders.

Another method is going on a foreign business trip. By this method, traders go to the destination and use the local trade association or commercial chambers, or find dealers from a telephone book, then meet the partners. Sometimes they make an educated guess about possible traders before going to the place. Making a business trip can be more effective in achieving an agreement. However, since it can be very costly while available partners are limited, direct visiting is usually the last stage of the process in making a final confirmation of the partner.

Each method has a different budget and has both positive and negative effects. In practice, traders combine several methods for each transaction to cover up any problems that may occur. When doing a transaction for the first time, methods that are disreputable should be avoided. Selecting methods is a basic key factor that will lead to good business matching where trust and progress can be achieved.

Except when doing transaction face to face, a common practice is to list up the appropriated dealers, send a transaction application and invite transaction. In such application forms, how the partner came to be known, a self-introduction and the expected transaction contents are included. Moreover, the transaction bank's name and transaction dealers' name are written as a credit reference of the company. At the stage, it is advised to invite assertively, by sending the catalog, price list and sample.

3 Credit Inquiry

3-1 Necessity of Credit Inquiry

After sending out an invitation and a favorable reply is received, the transaction can be concluded. At this stage, a credit inquiry should be made. International transactions are more complex compared with domestic transactions since the partner's credit standing is difficult to acknowledge. The risk of war, strike, and natural disaster is also much higher. Moreover, the government of each country enacts different policies on export and import. Due to these reasons, international business may not be as smooth as it appears and traders will face unexpected problems such as goods not being delivered, the fees not being paid, and claims.

The institutions of trade insurance and letter of credit can reduce such risks to some extent. However, it would be unnecessary to take measures to avoid risks if traders make transactions with a reliable partner who knows the target market well. In this way, claims concerning the contract can be avoided and the cost will be reduced.

In practice, a credit inquiry is always made in the first transaction. However, as politics and economies change, it is better to do the inquiry even though the transaction is proceeding smoothly.

3-2   Contents of Credit Inquiry

Credit inquiry is an investigation on the credibility of an organization that is to become one's business partner. Credit inquiry is composed of four elements known as the 4C, which are character, capacity, capital, and condition. Character refers to the commercial morality of an organization, namely the management style, honesty, attitude, and so on. Capacity refers to the management and business ability of an organization or the managers. Capacity is evaluated based on the scale, sales, business size, profit rate and growth rate. Capital refers to a set condition, details of the financial resources, property and debts. Condition refers to the environment in which the company is situated. This includes whether or not there is a regulation on export and import in the target market and what the regulations are. It also refers to conditions of the market and the goods transacted.

The importance of personal character is that it helps reduce unexpected risks and betters the transaction process. Even if some problems occur, it will be easier to solve them by cooperating with the partner. In this aspect, character is really important and should be taken into consideration when planning a new transaction. Capacity and capital change over time so traders should investigate them regularly even though the transaction has lasted for a long time. Conditions are easily accessed from newspaper, magazine and TV news. Information on the political and economic condition of the partner's country and the market condition can be found easily.

3-3   Access of Credit Inquiry

In the reply to the transaction invitation, usually the Bank Reference and Trade Reference are written. Traders can request for a credit inquiry. Nevertheless, banks hardly give out much information in order to keep official secrets. Information is not always given even when the name of the bank is introduced by the partner.

Traders can get information about credit inquiry. The bank

possesses an alliance overseas correspondent bank for remittance and foreign exchange transaction. The alliance bank is called a correspondent bank. In general, a bank will ask the correspondent banks located in the partner's area to do the credit inquiry. The correspondent banks provide credit information based on the credit ledger. With this information, the bank opinion will be written as an overall opinion by the bank. The banks will not charge extra charges except for the actual expense spent during the investigation.

The credit inquiry given by banks is reliable but does not contain much of the information on character and capacity. Thus, an inquiry should be made through a company in the same field. However, a report made by the dealer, who is introduced by the partner, is not objective. If possible, it is better to do a credit inquiry through the company's network.

Detailed and accurate information is needed when transacting a great amount or in a long-term transaction. Using specialized institutions (Mercantile Credit Agency) to make the credit inquiry is the most effective method. Though this may be costly, detailed information can be expected. JETRO is one of the organizations that provide a credit inquiry for trade promotion and it gives a discount for medium and small companies. A trader can request the Chamber of Commerce to source out the credit inquiry as well. Moreover, the Japan Trade Insurance provides a credit inquiry service based on the Overseas Business Firms List.

4   Engagement on General Terms and Conditions
4-1   Necessity of General Terms and Conditions
If there are no problems in the credit inquiry, an agreement on the general terms and conditions should be made before signing the contract. What are general terms and conditions and why is it important? International trade is transacted in countries with different

cultures, customs, languages, climate, and so on. These differences sometimes cause various kinds of problems.

Yet, time and cost is wasted if detailed conditions are agreed upon each time when transacting with the same partner. Here, some overall conditions that are not related with every single delivery will be agreed on before signing each individual contract. This is called general terms and conditions. The general terms and conditions will be printed on the back of the contract. That is why it is also called back provision or printed provision.

General terms and conditions are the conditions other than the specific terms and conditions that are determined individually during each delivery. Specific terms and conditions are about concrete items such as what, how much, how many, when, method of payment, insurance conditions and so on. They are indispensable that the transaction cannot be carried out when one is missing; they are also regarded as minimum conditions.

When negotiating the general terms and conditions, the exporter and importer send their terms and conditions to the other for further discussion. Though the conditions of both sides can be used, it is better to use one's own. In fact, general terms and conditions are rarely made in the actual negotiation, especially when the transaction is to be done in a hurry or to be made once. One needs to be cautious as negligence in the general terms and conditions would cause trouble in the contract. At least in the case of long term transactions, a concrete content of terms and conditions should be made in which general terms and conditions are included.

4-2 Agency and Distributorship Agreements

When the exporter appoints the importer as a sale agent or distributor, or when the importer appoints the exporter as a buying agent; a different type of contract called Agency Agreement or Distributorship Agreement is to be made.

Again, what are agents and distributors? In transaction, both sides appoint the other side as its agent or distributor. Without this appointment, they cannot be an agent or distributor; they cannot be called a distributor only by selling the products of the principals.

A distributor buys the product, makes an inventory and resells with its own money and risk. Its profit is the difference between the purchasing amount and resale amount. This is called a margin. The agent finds a place for stocking and purchasing, and then signs the contract. The nominal participant of the contract is the one who appointed the agent. That is to say, the agent only signs the contract. The return on the agent is a certain percentage of the contract fee. This is called a commission. In practice, this commission based transaction, refers to the transaction based on an agent contract.

There can be two patterns of contracts. One is to sign a contract with one's own name. These kinds of dealers are called principals; distributors are principals. The other pattern is to sign a contract for someone else; this is an agent. Here, the contents of an agency and distributorship contract will not be explained. Please refer to related reference books for more details.

4-3 Content of General Terms and Conditions
4-3-1 Transaction Basis
Please look at Form 1 when reading this explanation. The first item is the transaction form. The Principal-to-Principal Basis mentioned here refers to a non-agent-transaction. As mentioned earlier, there are two patterns of contracts; appointing an agent and an independent dealers' transaction as principals. Here, the transaction is one between independent dealers. In the general terms and conditions, rarely is there a regulation on agent transaction. In the case of an agent transaction, a special agent contract is necessary.

A distributor is also a kind of principal although the principal mentioned here does not include the distributor. It is because a special distributor contract is also necessary in the case of a distributor.

4-3-2   Quantity and Quality

It is determined here that the exporter takes responsibility for quantity. This is usually made up by two conditions. One is shipped quantity terms in which an exporter certifies the quantity until shipping. The other one is landed quantity terms in which the quantity is guaranteed until unloading. Guarantee on quality is also made until shipping and until unloading. In practice, quantity can be checked by some method; however, no method for quality check exists since the check by the factory before shipping is the last check. Thus, it is regulated here that the factory's check is the final one.

Special regulations are not necessarily made here since trade terms regulate until when the exporter should be responsible for quantity and quality. For example, it is regulated by FOB, C&F and CIF, which are usually used, that the delivery place is the shipping place, so the exporter should also guarantee quantity and quality until shipping. Yet, when a place other than the one determined in the trade terms is to be a guarantee limitation place, a special regulation is to be made. At this time, as specific condition is superior to a general condition, specific conditions must be written on the surface.

Moreover, it is regulated that if the importer demands that the exporter inspects the quality, the exporter should do it for the importer in addition to the one done before. There are two kinds of inspection; one is general inspection and the other is specific inspection. The former one is obligatory since it is written in contract, and the latter one is needed when the importer requires it in the import place for a special reason. In this case, the importer should pay for it.

For some goods, no profit can be earned without a certain number of sales. In such occasions, a Minimum Quantity Acceptable is regulated. When sales are limited, a Maximum Quantity Acceptable is stipulated.

Form 1: General Terms and Conditions

GENERAL TERMS AND CONDITIONS

1. **TRANSACTION BASIS**
   All business is transacted between Seller and Buyer on a principal-to-principal basis.

2. **QUANTITY AND QUALITY**
   Unless other specified, the shipping weight and /or count at the time and place of shipping shall be final. The factory's quality inspection shall also be final. If Buyer requests Seller, Seller shall make special inspection on Buyer's account.

3. **PAYMENT**
   If and when Buyer is to establish a letter of credit in favor of Seller, Buyer shall establish it through a prime bank immediately after the conclusion of this Contract.

4. **SHIPMENT**
   Unless otherwise specified on the face hereof, partial shipment and/or transshipment are permitted. In case of FOB, FCA or other similar terms under which Buyer has to contract for carriage, Seller may, if requested by Buyer, contract for carriage on usual terms at Buyer's risk and expense.

5. **INSURANCE**
   Unless otherwise specified on the face hereof, Seller shall, in case of CIF or CIP, insure the cargo on Institute Cargo Clauses (A) including War & S. R. C. C. risks for 110 % of the invoice amount.

6. **CLAIM**
   Buyer shall file a claim regarding the cargo with Seller in writing within ten (10) days after receipt of the Goods at the destination. No claim can be filed when the Goods are used.

7. **INTELLECTUAL PROPERTY**
   Buyer shall hold Seller harmless from and waive any claim against Seller for any alleged infringement regarding patent, utility model, trademark, design and copyright in the Goods.

8. **WARRANTY**
   Unless otherwise specified on the face hereof, Seller makes no warranty, express or implied, as to the fitness and suitability of the goods for any particular purpose and/or merchantability.

9. **FORCE MAJEURE**
   Seller shall not be responsible for the delay in shipment due directly or indirectly to force majeure including mobilization, war, riots, civil commotions, hostilities, blockade, requisition of vessels, prohibition of export, fires, floods, earthquakes, tempests, strikes, lockouts and any other contingencies which prevent shipment within the period stipulated. In case of force majeure, the time of shipment shall be extended for fifteen (15) days. It shall be at Seller's option whether or not the contract will be cancelled if such force majeure continues after the end of the extended period.

10. **ARBITRATION**
    Any dispute or claim arising out of or relating to this Contract shall be finally settled by arbitration in Japan, in accordance with the Commercial Arbitration Rules of the Japan Commercial Arbitration Association. The award rendered by the arbitrators shall be final and binding upon both parties concerned.

11. **ENTIRE AGREEMENT**
    The Contract shall constitute the entire and only agreement between Seller and Buyer with respect to the subject matter hereof and supersede, cancel and annul all prior agreement.

12. **TRADE TERMS AND GOVERNING LAW**
    The trade terms used herein shall be governed and interpreted by the provisions of INCOTERMS 2000 (ICC Pub.No.560). The formation, validity, construction and performance of this Contract shall be governed by and construed in accordance with the laws of Japan.

4-3-3 Payment

There are times when a concrete payment method regulates payment; this will be determined in specific terms and regulations. Here, it is only regulated that it should be immediately issued by first-class banks when the letter of credit (L/C) is used.

The L/C is issued by the importer's bank to the exporter for certifying the importer's payment. In transaction using the L/C, payment will be guaranteed if the contract procedure is under the L/C conditions. However, since the issuance of the L/C is always delayed in practice, it tends to be issued by banks of lower liability. In this regulation, it is demanded that the L/C be issued immediately and that it be issued by banks of high liability.

4-3-4 Shipment

At first, the exporter must decide whether to accept partial shipment or transshipment. In partial shipment, goods provided by one contract will be delivered several times. Transshipment requires that the loaded goods be transferred from one ship to another before reaching the destination. Both partial shipment and transshipment are accepted here.

For trade terms such as the FOB, where the importer arranges the transport, the exporter is to carry out the arrangements of transport instead. It is regulated here that the exporter can sign a transport contract for sharing the importer's risk and cost burden.

4-3-5 Insurance

Insurance refers to cargo insurance. Based on the trade terms, the exporter must obtain cargo insurance only when using CIF or CIP. Regulation is made on insurance conditions, special risks and insurance amount.

The insurance conditions mentioned here are the All Risks condition; special risks are War & S.R.C.C. Risks guarantee and the insurance amount is 10% more than the contract amount. A concrete explanation will be made on the specific terms and conditions of cargo insurance. Please refer to the chapter on cargo insurance.

4-3-6 Claim

Claim refers to one of the parties requiring compensation from the other if the quality didn't match what was written in the contract or if there was any damage or if payment was not made. Claim can be referred to as a complaint in which no compensation requirement is involved. However, complaint and claim totally differ in law.

Regulations are made in general terms and conditions on the time duration and method of making an accusation. If the cargo is damaged, a survey report should also be submitted. It is regulated here that the claim must be brought in writing within ten days after the cargo's arrival in the import place. If the cargo is used, the claim is considered invalid.

Quality defect includes patent defect and latent defect. Since the defect cannot be detected until use in latent defect, the claim time is much longer and sometimes the last article is deleted.

4-3-7 Intellectual Property

Intellectual property includes patent right, utility model right, trademark right, design right and copyright. Patent right is the right for a new technique. Utility model right is the right for the application of existing technology. Trademark right is the right for a trademark and style. Design right is the right for designing a letter. Copyright is the right of publications, computer program and so on.

Dispute on intellectual property often occurs in the import country. In other words, the imported product violates another's right in the import country. At this time, the importer is the person concerned and he will be accused or be asked to compensate. Thus, the exporter is not considered to be responsible for the dispute.

However, for the importer, an exporter's exporting goods that violate intellectual property can be considered as a breach of contract. For this reason, the exporter is responsible for the dispute most of the time.

4-3-8　Warranty

Most conflicts between the exporter and the importer are on the quality of the goods. A warranty is an article which guarantees the seller's product responsibility. Here, it is regulated that if without specific regulations, the seller does not guarantee, either explicitly or implicitly, the goods' adaptability for special purposes and merchantability.

Without specific regulation, it is required that the quality of the goods match the sample or the pamphlet in the contract negotiation. The problem is the guarantee on the product value when the buyer resells them and when the buyer uses it for one's own special purpose. The seller must make sure to avoid such a guarantee. On the contrary, the buyer cares about the latent defect when using or reselling. Although one method is to prolong the claim duration, it is desired that such defects are considered in the warranty article.

4-3-9　Force Majeure

There are occasions when the seller cannot transfer the goods to the buyer for some reasons. The article of force majuere lists the reasons in which the seller's responsibility can be exempted. It is also regulated here how much time can be extended if delivery is not made in time and whether the contract should be terminated if the cargo is not delivered even after the time has been prolonged. It is regulated here that the time can be extended to 15 days and that the seller can cancel the contract if the cargo is not delivered after the prolonged time.

The seller and buyer always have different ideas on what the force majuere is; therefore, it is necessary that concrete and detailed regulations are determined. Mostly, the items that are not written in the contract are not regarded as force majuere.

4-3-10　Arbitration

It is regulated here that the final measure used to solve the battle is arbitration. The place of arbitration, the arbitration institute and arbitration rules are set here as the three Principles of Arbitration. There is also one measure for a court lawsuit. Both methods have advantages and disadvantages and its usage is determined depending on the occasion. This will be explained in detail in the chapter on "Claim"; please refer to it for specific ideas.

4-3-11 Entire Agreement

Various agreements are reached during the negotiation. Sometimes a dispute occurs since the agreement made earlier is different from what was written in the contract or the contents discussed are not included in the contract. It is regulated here that the contents in the contract are what has been agreed upon no matter what agreement is reached later.

When there are many transaction contents, a document called the Letter of Intent is signed and exchanged for each transaction item. Although the content of the Letter of Intent will be reflected in the final contract, sometimes the contents of the two do not match. In this case, if there is a complete agreement in the contract, the contract will be considered as superior.

4-3-12 Trade Terms and Governing Law

It is regulated here what kind of international rules are used as the standard definitions of trade terms and which country's law is to be used as the base law for the entire contract.

Incoterms, made by the International Commerce Chamber, will be the international standard for trade terms definitions. Incoterms is revised every ten years. One is free to determine which version to use, but it is common to use the latest version. Contract conclusion, validity and contents should be determined by one country's law which is called the governing law. The country can be the export country, the import country, or even a third country.

4-4 Battle of Forms

General terms and conditions are rarely made when a transaction is done in one time or done in a hurry. Usually in this case, the transaction is carried out with specific terms and conditions immediately after finding the partner. After an agreement is reached, the buyer or seller makes the contract. On the surface of the contract, the specific terms and conditions are printed; on the back of the contract, the advantageous content is printed. After making two copies of the contract, both are sent to the partner for them to sign and return one of the copies.

Some conditions cannot be agreed upon in the contract sent because they are advantageous for the partner. In this case, two copies need to be signed again. The contracts are sent and one copy must be returned. Then there will be two kinds of unsigned contract; four pieces in all. After signing the contract sent by the partner, the disadvantageous conditions will be deleted and sent back; it may be sent back with additions of advantageous conditions.

This is called the battle of forms. Even if the contract is not signed, in most cases the contract is executed as if nothing happened. However, since this will cause conflict, it is vital to pay attention to the following points in order not to have any disadvantages. Firstly, conclude general terms and conditions if possible, and use one's own company's form as a tentative plan. If general terms and conditions are not made, send the contract immediately to the partner after making specific terms and conditions. After receiving the contract from the partner, read the general terms and conditions carefully, delete any problems and send it back.

Questions

1 Explain the importance of credit inquiry, inquiry items and methods.
2 Explain the necessity of general terms and conditions.
3 Compare and explain the transaction by an agent and transaction by oneself.
4 Discuss in class the measures for avoiding contract conflicts.

Chapter 2
Price Quotation and Trade Terms

Summary

After finding a reliable partner and concluding general terms and conditions, concrete contract conditions must be negotiated. The main issue of negotiation is the quality and price of the goods. In this chapter, quality determining methods and price estimation will be explained. When estimating the price, trade terms must be determined as a calculation basis. Trade terms will be explained later in this chapter.

1 Negotiation on Quality and Price

1-1 Ways of Determining Quality

After an agreement is reached on the general terms and conditions, negotiations are to be carried out on specific terms and conditions. If general ones are not made, specific ones are to be negotiated immediately after finding a partner.

In a transaction negotiation, negotiation materials such as catalog, pamphlet, sample, and price list are used. It is better for the seller to send the negotiation materials together with the transaction proposal. Such negotiation materials are used to determine the cost of different goods. The quality and price are the main objective for negotiations.

First of all, the ways of determining quality will be explained. As shown in Figure 2, the two major categories are sale by sample and sale by description. Sale by description includes sale by specification, sale by standard, sale by grade and sale by brand or trade mark.

Sale by sample is a method in which the quality is determined by a sample. The principle is that the quality of goods delivered must match that of the sample. A claim could be made if the quality differs. For this reason, it is important for the seller to keep a duplicate sample or triplicate sample when sending the original sample to the buyer, in order to prepare for a claim.

Figure 2   Ways of determining quality

- Sale by Sample
- Sale by Description

- Sale by Specification
- Sale by Standard
- Sale by Grade
- Sale by Brand or Trade Mark

If the buyer's sample is sent by the buyer, the seller should make a similar sample and send it to the buyer as a counter sample to get consent. With this procedure, a claim from the buyer can be avoided. If the quality of goods is not able to match that of the sample, the article, "sample and real goods are not always matched" should be written into the general terms and conditions.

In the case of big facilities or factory equipment of which samples cannot be made, plans, illustrations, photos, data are used to demonstrate the quality. This is called sale by specifications. If concrete items cannot all be written in the contract in this sale by specifications, the specification itself is attached to the contract.

For natural resources and agricultural products, a standard for quality is used. This standard is applied to determine quality. This is called sale by standard. For example, the USQ (Usual Standard Quality) demonstrates the standards made by public organizations; GMQ (Good Merchantable Quality) demonstrates sellable quality for wood and frozen fishes; and FAQ (Fair Average Quality) demonstrates the average quality in a year for grain.

In products whose grade is widely known internationally, the quality is determined by the grades. This is called sale by grade. Some examples include ISO by International Organization for Standardization, IEC by international Electro-technical Commission and JIS (Japanese Industrial Standard).

If the products are widely known, the brand name and model number can be used to determine the quality. Such methods, where the quality is determined by the brand or trademark, are called sale by brand or trademark.

1-2　Price list

Negotiation on price requires time and effort. The item used as a negotiation material is the price list. There are lists printed as pamphlets which record the prices of all the goods, made for unspecified negotiation partners. There are lists made for specified partners. The former one is called a fixed price list and the latter one is called quotations. Form 2 shows the example of the latter one. In the price list, the expected contract terms are also written besides the item name and price in order to promote the partner's assertive purchasing activity. As the price may fluctuate, the article, "the prices are subject to market fluctuations" should be written. Other contract terms can also be written for reference.

In Form 2, the minimum quantity, payment conditions, packing and shipment are written. "E. & O.E." written in the bottom left is the abbreviation for "Error and Omissions are Excepted", meaning that even if something is wrong or omitted in the price list, responsibility is not taken.

There are occasions when a proforma invoice, instead of a price list, is made and sent to the buyer. In a proforma invoice, the item, quantity and delivery time are written more specifically than they are in the price list. Sometimes they are also used as a contract in itself after

Form 2: Price List

JAPAN TRADING CO., LTD.

3-8-5 Shibuya, Shibuya-ku
Tokyo 150-0021
JAPAN

TEL: 03-3797-4567
FAX: 03-3797-5678

7 April, 20--

Manukau Trading Co., Ltd.
893 Dickson Ave.
Auckland

PRICE LIST No. 1

ITEM NO.	DESCRIPTION	UNIT PRICE FOB TOKYO
TKC-8890	Portable CD System PMSE 3	US$398.00
TKC-8891	Portable CD System PMSE 5	US$410.00
TKC-2345	Micro CD System PMSF 8	US$510.00
TKC-2346	Micro CD System PMSF 9	US$540.00

REMARKS
1) The above prices are on the basis of FOB Tokyo and subject to market fluctuations.
2) Minimum quantity: 3 dozen for each item
3) Draft at sight under irrevocable L/C
4) Packing: One dozen in a case
5) Shipment: 30 days after receipt of L/C

JAPAN TRADING CO., LTD.
(*Signed*)
Export Manager

E. & O. E.

Figure 3   Trade transaction cost

Export Packing	Has inner and outer package. Conventional ship requires higher fee than container ship. This fee is included in the prime cost when stocked from the domestic maker.
Export place Transport	When stocked by the domestic maker into warehouses in the export port, the fee is included in the prime cost.
Export customs entry	The export customs entry fee, fee paid to Customs clearance dealer is included.
Shipment	Treatment fee to the forwarder, preservation fee, container loading fee, piling fee, inspection fee are included.
Bank	Post fee when sending documentary bill from export place to import place; interest and service charge when using trade finance.
International Transport	Marine transport fee, air transport fee and combined transport fee are included.
Cargo Insurance	Not only in international transport, but in domestic as well if necessary.
Import customs entry	The fee includes import duty, consumption tariff and other clearance fee. Fee paid to Customs clearance dealer is counted as well.
Unloading	In addition to the fee paid to the forwarder, container clearing fee, container drawing fee, preservation fee and shipping fee are included.
Import place Transport	Sometimes the container itself is carried to warehouse from the port and sometimes goods are drawn out of the container and then moved, respectively called dray fee and delivery fee.

the buyer has agreed. Moreover, they are also used as documents for temporary customs clearance in the import place.

1-3 Price Quotation

Figure 3 shows the cost during trade transaction. More costs are involved for transaction of special goods. In general, however, only the cost written in this figure is to be paid.

There are two methods of price calculation. The Cost Plus Method is to add on the necessary cost to the primary cost.
The other method, the Break Down Method, determines the cost by estimating the marketing conditions. The latter one is often used when marketing joining and expanding marketing share is considered a priority.

When quoting prices, it should be determined which fee is to be paid by the seller and which is to be paid by the buyer. In domestic transaction, the seller usually hands over the goods to the buyer, meaning that the seller pays the cost until the goods are delivered to the buyer in his warehouse.

However, in trade transaction, trade terms determine which of the two pays the cost. It is shown by abbreviations such as FOB, CIF, C&F, etc.

2 Trade Terms

2-1 The Function of Trade Terms

In the trading transaction, there are a great amount of expenses when the goods are transferred from an exporting country to the importing country. The cost cannot be determined only by the indicated price. The price cannot be estimated without clarifying to what extent the seller is responsible for the cost, and from where the buyer must take the responsibility.

Trade terms determine this type of division of costs. As in such a transaction as US$120,000 FOB Kobe, the price is followed by the name of the port and the name of the place. The trade terms used are also stated as part of the fundamental price calculation.

Trade terms show the divisions between the costs of the seller and the buyer. However, trade terms have more functions. For example, they indicate the place and the method of delivery. Also, they help to identify where the seller transfers his responsibilities of ownership and risk liabilities to the buyer. In other words, trade terms specify the overall condition of the delivery of goods and can be referred to as delivery terms.

Firstly, trade terms show the division of costs. In trading transaction, trade terms are always written after the price; therefore, it is understood that the terms being used are based on the price estimation. On the contrary, the cost cannot be determined as being high or low if trade terms are not written. In practice, the division of costs is the most important. Therefore, it is crucial to understand clearly where to divide the costs responsibly for each trade terms.

Next, trade terms show the place and the method of delivery. Although each trade terms have its own delivery place, they can generally be classified into the shipment contract and the destination contract. The delivery place of goods for the shipment contract is at the export port. The destination contract is made at the import port.

There are two methods of delivery. One method is the actual delivery where delivery is considered completed when the goods have been delivered. The other method is called the symbolic delivery. It is considered completed when the securities that are issued at the port are passed to the buyer. So far, FOB is considered as actual delivery and CIF as symbolic delivery. However, a bill of lading, which is a document of title is used even in actual delivery but is considered as symbolic delivery. It is also difficult to consider a method to be symbolic delivery if a negotiable transport document is not used. It is very difficult to distinguish both delivery methods in each trade terms. Therefore, in this chapter, we only need to understand that there are two methods of delivery.

Lastly, trade terms reveal the proprietary rights and the division of risk liability. Proprietorship is the right to make free use of the goods or the right to dispose the goods. Likewise, risk liability means that either the seller or buy must take responsibility when the goods are damaged or lost.

Up until now, the idea of risk liability being transferred according to the move of proprietorship has been very common. However, the theory of transferring proprietorship is very difficult to understand. It is rare for the transfer of proprietary rights to become a problem. For this reason, when people think of proprietorship and risk liability together, the problem of transferring risk liability only becomes complicated. Since that has proved meaningless, recently, people differentiate proprietorship and risk liability and have neglected the problem of transferring proprietorship. At this stage, we only need to understand the time of transferring of risks for each trade term.

In conclusion, when we learn about trade terms, we only need to understand the transfer of cost, delivery place, and transfer of risk.

2-2   International Standard Rules of Trade Terms

By using trade terms, a trade transaction can be carried out rationally. However, if the seller and buyer do not come to an agreement with the interpretation, it would result in a dispute. It will also delay the growth of the trading business.

Therefore, there were attempts to unify the interpretation of trade terms. First, in 1919, the U.S. Overseas Trading Council made a principle called the American Foreign Trade Definition. Then, with the cooperation of the International Chamber of Commerce, International Law Association maked the Warsaw Oxford Rules in 1932. This rule has interpreted CIF in detail. In 1941, the U.S. Overseas Trading

Council revised the American Foreign Trade Definition and came to be called the Revised American Foreign Trade Definition 1941.

Although International Chamber of Commerce (ICC) had participated in the making of the Warsaw Oxford Rules, the ICC maked the International Commercial Terms, known as Incoterms, with the aim for it to be used widely around the world. Afterwards, revisions were made in the years of 1956, 1967, 1976, 1980, 1990 and 2000. It is used as a base principle in many contracts because of how it has been revised diligently, it has a wide range of adopted terms, and the text can be easily understood. Figure 4 shows the revised edition of Incoterms 2000 and explains the established conditions in Incoterms 2000. There are 13 conditions, which are classified into four types (E type, F type, G type and H type). The order of explanation slightly differs from the table.

Table 4   Incoterms 2000

Type E (Place of shipment)	EXW	Ex Works
Type F (Buyer bears main cost and freight)	FCA	Free Carrier
	FAS	Free Alongside Ship
	FOB	Free On Board
Type C (Seller bears main costs and freight)	CFR	Cost and Freight
	CIF	Cost, Insurance and Freight
	CPT	Carriage Paid To
	CIP	Carriage and Insurance Paid to
Type D (Arrival place)	DAF	Delivered At Frontier
	DES	Delivered Ex Ship
	DEQ	Delivered Ex Quay
	DDU	Delivered Duty Unpaid
	DDP	Delivered Duty Paid

2-3　Terms of Incoterms
2-3-1　EXW (Ex Works...specified place)

This condition means that the seller delivers when he places the goods at the disposal of the buyer at the seller's premises or another place that is not cleared for export. The condition is that delivery is made at the place where the goods exist. The name of the place is written after EXW. Works are the facilities where the goods are placed such as the mill, the warehouse, the plant, the plantation, the mine, godown, and so on.

The exporter conducts the export packaging that suits the delivery means and must print shipping and care marks on the packing. The exporter should pay all costs until they have been delivered. He must pay the expenses for quality inspection and packing. Risk transfers when the goods are handed over. It is the condition in which the seller has the least expense responsibility.

The keyword of EXW is "existing place of the goods." It can be understood as transferring the goods, the expenses and the risks there.

2-3-2　FAS (Free alongside Ship... port of export)

In this condition, the delivery is completed when the goods are delivered at the pier of the port for loading or at the barge at the side of vessel. The exporter delivers the goods that are placed alongside the vessel at the named port of shipment. The named port of shipment is written after FAS. The risk is transferred when the goods are delivered alongside the vessel. This condition is used in inland waterway transportation where the seller is in control of the goods at the side of the vessel, if is a traditional ship. FAS is used only for traditional vessels and not for container ships.

The exporter should bear all costs including customs clearance expenses until the goods are delivered. The keyword of FAS is "alongside the vessel".

2-3-3 FOB (Free on Board... port of export)

In these terms, the exporter delivers the goods on the ship at the named port of shipment. The delivery is regarded as completed when the goods are passed through the rail of the ship. Risks will also be transferred from the seller to the buyer at that moment. The exporter is responsible for the expense of export packing, domestic transportation, customs clearance and loading. The buyer also has to make arrangements for international transportation and take responsibility for additional expenses after loading.

In FOB, the goods are handed over on the vessel. Therefore, it must be used only in the condition that the seller can control the goods through shipment on board the vessel. In this case, all vessels other than container ships are used. In a container ship, the cargo is delivered to the carrier before loading so theoretically FOB cannot be used.

The buyer has to contract for international transport in FOB. However, it is inconvenient for the buyer, who is in the import place, to arrange for transportation at the export place. In this case, it is possible for the buyer to ask the seller to carry it out on behalf of the buyer. When this happens, the seller has to contract for carriage while the buyer pays the freight at the port of import.

The keyword for FOB is "on board." The delivery is carried out on board where the expenses and risks are transferred.

2-3-4 FCA (Free Carrier...specified place)

In FOB delivery is made on board the vessel. This is based on the premises that the exporter has authority at the designated port and can take responsibility until loading. At present, most sea transport is by container ship. However, in container transport, the goods are passed to the container collection facility like a container yard before loading the freight. It is the terms of FCA that Incoterms adopted for container vessels or the same loading methods like air transport.

First of all, the place of delivery of FCA is the place where the goods are passed to the forwarder or his agent before loading.

Generally, in Japan, this is the container yard, freight station and such places at the port. The names of these places are to be written after FCA. For air transport, the goods are to be passed to the airline's agent at the forwarder's storage near the airport.

In the division of costs, the exporter is responsible for all costs from completing the custom clearance to handing over the goods to the carrier or its agent. The importer is responsible for the costs of international freight and the cargo insurance premium. Risk is transferred when the cargo is handed over to the carrier.

The keyword for FCA is "handing over to the carrier." The responsibility of expenses is the same as FOB, but the loading place is from the board to the land. Therefore, FCA is referred to as "FOB of surface delivery."

2-3-5   CFR (Cost and Freight... port of import)

These terms are generally abbreviated as C&F. In Incoterms, it is abbreviated as CFR for the purposes of computer communication so that people do not need to use the shift key when typing CFR. The name of the import port is written after the terms. The word cost in cost and freight refers to the FOB Cost.

The condition for CFR is that the seller can afford the FOB cost added onto the international freight. The exporter delivers the goods when they pass the ship's rail in the port of shipment. This is only used in traditional vessels where the seller can be responsible for the goods until the transaction is completed at the ship's rail. Risk is transferred at the port of shipment. The "costs" is the FOB costs.

The delivery of CFR is a little complicated. A bill of landing is necessary and must be handed over to the buyer. This is Symbolic Delivery. In principle, the transport document used must include a document of title. In Incoterms 2000, transport documents, which could not be negotiable, were recognized. If possible, negotiable documents should be used.

The risk is transferred when the freight is passed at the ship's rail of the vessel at the export port. Theoretically, CFR cannot be used for a container vessel. The keyword for CFR is "freight."

2-3-6 CIF (Cost, Insurance and Freight... port of import)

In CIF, the seller has to be responsible for insurance arrangement. The name of the import port is written after it. The seller must apply for international transport and pay for the freight and the insurance premium. The seller has to present the insurance policy to the buyer. The seller delivers the goods when they pass the ship's rail. He makes the contracts for insurance and transport. All additional costs after shipment must be born by the importer. This is only for the traditional vessel.

If the terms of insurance cannot be agreed upon, the minimum condition of FPA or ICC (C) is sufficient. If the buyer asks for an extraneous risk, it will be on the buyer's account. In trade terms, CIF is the only terms where the seller is obligated to insure the cargo for the buyer.

As in CFR, delivery is symbolic one as well. Not only the seller hands over the cargo over the rail of the ship, but also he must provide the document of title like a B/L to the buyer. In the case of CIF, offering the insurance policy and negotiable document become an obligation. As mentioned before, it is recommendable to use a negotiable document as in CFR.

The transfer of risk occurs at the ship's rail at the port of export. For this reason, it cannot be used for a container ship, and the seller must use a traditional vessel where one can control the cargo until loading.

The keyword for CIF is "freight and insurance premium."

2-3-7 CPT (Carriage Paid To ...port of import)

In these terms, the exporter pays all costs until delivery before shipment and freight to the destination. Delivery usually takes place at the container yard or the container station at the port of shipment. This is for air and container transportation and is equivalent to CFR in the division of costs. The destination of transport is written after CPT. As described above, delivery is made before shipment. This usually happens at the CY (container yard) or the CFS (container freight station) near the port of export. For the division of costs, the exporter bears all costs until delivery including carriage. The risks are transferred to the importer as the goods are delivered to the carrier.

The keyword for CPT is "delivered to the carrier" and "freight."

2-3-8 CIP (Carriage and Insurance Paid To... port of import)

These are the terms that insurance premium is on the exporter in addition to CPT. The exporter delivers the goods to the carrier appointed by him; in addition, he must pay insurance premium. The transport destination is written after CIP. The exporter must deliver the goods to the carrier. These terms are the same as FCA and CPT and are used in all the transport modes as long as delivery is carried out to the carrier before shipment such as the container vessel and air transport.

The division of costs is the same as CIF. The time of delivery is the delivery to the carrier before shipping. That is why it is also called "CIF of surface delivery."

The keyword for CIP is "deliver to the carrier" and "freight and insurance premium."

2-3-9 DAF (Delivered At Frontier...specified place)

These terms are only used between nations sharing the same border. The exporter bears all costs until the goods are delivered at the named place at the frontier. The seller is responsible for export customs entry and the buyer is responsible for import customs entry. The risks are also transferred from the seller to the buyer at that time. The keyword for DAF is "frontier".

2-3-10 DES (Delivered Ex Ship...named port of import)

The exporter delivers the goods to the importer on board the vessel at the named port of destination. The importer must bear all costs and risks involved in unloading the goods to the named port of destination. The keyword for DES is "on board the vessel at the import port."

2-3-11 DEQ (Delivered Ex Quay... port of import)

The exporter delivers the goods to the importer without going through import customs entry on the quay at the named port of destination. The importer has to bear the costs of import customs entry. The keyword for DEQ is "quay at the named port of destination."

2-3-12 DDU (Delivered Duty Unpaid... port of import)

The exporter delivers the goods to the buyer at the named place of destination without unloading the goods from the means of transportation. The exporter has to bear the costs and risks involved in bringing the goods there. The importer has to bear the expenses of import customs entry and duties if necessary.

DDU is used when there is no import customs entry in an economically integrated market like EU or when foreigners are not permitted to clear the import custom according to the law.

The keyword for DDU is "not cleared for import and not unloaded from any means of transport at the named place of destination."

2-3-13 DDP (Delivered Duty Paid... port of import)

The exporter delivers the goods to the buyer at the named place of destination without unloading from any arriving means of transport. The exporter has to bear the costs and risks involved in bringing the goods there. The exporter has to bear expenses for the import customs entry as well.

The keyword for DDP is "cleared for import and not unloaded from any means of transport at the named place of destination".

2-4 Terms Used in Practice

In conclusion, FOB, C&F, and CIF are the most common terms used in both import and export and by sea or air.

It is now the era of container and air transport. Incoterms explains that FOB, C&F and CIF are used for the traditional ship where the exporter can be responsible for the goods until they are loaded on board the ship. In relation to the risk division in FOB, C&F and CIF, they cannot be used in container or air transport. Instead, new terms (FCA, CPT and CIP) are introduced. For FCA, CPT, and CIP in air and container transport, the exporter cannot be responsible for the goods on board the ship since he has to hand in the goods to the carrier before shipment. However, these are not used often.

Another fact we have to consider is that although CFR is being used as an abbreviation in Incoterms, in practice, C&F is used instead of CFR. In fact, most of the terms in the contracts are regulated as "according to the explanation of trade terms". However, in actual practice, it seems to me that Incoterms is seldom used as a governing law. Considering the fact that there are many things that are not decided in the general terms and conditions, general terms and conditions themselves are seldom considered important.

Recently there is a report stating that terms where either the seller or the buyer takes charge of the transportation section are increasing as in EXF (Ex Factory), EXW, DDP and so on. From the perspective of logistics and for a more efficient distribution of goods, it is inconvenient to have a cut off in the transferring of the division of costs from the seller to the buyer.

We should pay attention to two conditions. One is whether changes should be made from the traditional trade terms to the new trade terms; another is that if the terms such as EXW or DDP will continue to increase from now on.

Questions

1 Explain how the quality of goods is determined in negotiation.
2 Explain the function of trade terms.
3 Please discuss in class how trade terms will be used from now on.

Chapter 3
Specific Terms and Conditions

Summary

First, we have to learn about the formation process of a contract. We need to understand that a sales contract is formed by offer and acceptance. Also, there are cases when a firm offer or order concludes an agreement. Next, we will study the content of a specific contract. The specific contract is the essence of trade transaction. All the conditions are very important, but if we understand payment in particular, we will be able to grasp a better understanding of transaction as a whole.

1   Formation of Sale Contract

1-1   Negotiation Process
After you have concluded the general terms and conditions, a more concrete negotiation is the next step. All the specific terms and conditions are brought to an agreement using negotiation materials such as sample, pamphlet, price list, and so forth.

The concrete conditions are the minimum requirement for carrying out an agreement; for each agreement there is a condition. For example, what kind of goods, how many, how much they cost, the date of delivery and method of payment are to be decided. It is the same as domestic transaction.

These kinds of concrete conditions are called specific terms and conditions. In some cases, you do not agree upon general terms and conditions and start to negotiate specific terms and conditions as soon as a negotiating partner is found. If they come to an agreement, the seller and buyer are under a contract relation; the seller carries out the duty to deliver the goods and the buyer has to make payment.

However, when and how do the buyer and the seller legally come to an agreement? This is achieved by offer and acceptance.

In negotiating a sales contract, the seller and the buyer have to discuss their demands. However, in the end, a contract is concluded when an offer is accepted with no conditions and modifications. A contract is also concluded when each condition is agreed upon and it comes to a point where there is no need to negotiate on additional terms.

This final decision is called acceptance and there are no conditions or modifications. The partner's will indication can be regarded as an offer.

When the will indication of acceptance is by mail, it becomes important to understand the timing of when the acceptance becomes effective. That is, a contract is concluded when the acceptance becomes effective. Principle of dispatch is reflected in Japanese and Anglo-Saxon civil law; and the Principle of arrival is reflected in German civil law and the Vienna Convention.

The last will indication is acceptance, which follows the offer. Before offer and acceptance, all prior negotiations are called preliminary negotiations.

1-2   Offer and Order

In actual practice, it is common to send offer forms, acceptance forms or order forms to conclude a contract.

In the practice of transaction and negotiation, as long as the buyer and the seller understand the terms and conditions, it is fine even if the specific terms and conditions are not clearly indicated. However, it is necessary to clarify the period of when the acceptance is effective because there is no internationally accepted interpretation of agreement for the acceptance in the form of letter. Besides, an offer cannot guarantee whether an acceptance is effective forever. It is hard to accept an offer made one or two years ago. Therefore, a sentence should be indicated in the offered paper: "We are pleased to make the following firm offer subject to your acceptance reaching us by the end of May." This is called a firm offer.

There are two meanings of firm offer. One is to clarify the definite period of acceptance. The other is to adopt the principle of arrival, which places importance on arrival.

In actual practice, there is offer subject to confirmation or offer subject to prior sale. Offer subject to confirmation means that the buyer accepts the seller's "offer", but the agreement can be drawn up after the final confirmation of the seller. This is used for goods whose market price fluctuates. If a buyer accepts a seller's "offer" unconditionally, the contract of sale is concluded. In practice, however, the first "offer" is rarely accepted; usually a buyer requests various conditions such as a discount.

This buyer's "offer" is called a "counter offer." When a seller or buyer accepts the other party's conditions through this exchange of "counter offers", the negotiation comes to an agreement.

There are occasions where an order is used instead of an offer letter or an acceptance letter. The buyer writes his necessary items onto the order form and sends it to the seller. Legally, is this an offer or acceptance?

It is possible to consider it as either an offer or acceptance. This is determined by the kind of transaction and how it proceeds. For example, after ordering, if a confirmation of order is sent, the order becomes an offer, and the confirmation of order becomes an acceptance. Likewise, if there is no confirmation of order, and the goods are automatically sent, then the order is considered an acceptance.

If risks are to be avoided, it is advisable to send the confirmation of order for an order. In that case, the order becomes an offer and when the order is not accepted, the contract will not be effective if a letter is sent saying that order cannot be accepted. In some cases in practice, the letters of offer and acceptance, or the order form and confirmation of order are usually sent by fax. However, these kinds of documents can possibly conclude a contract, and you should send the original contract by mail or courier. We should be cautious because the fax is regarded as a copy that has no validity.

1-3 Drafting Contract

It is necessary to exchange the contract after the specific terms and conditions have been agreed upon in a document or an oral negotiation. Likewise, there is a will of indication for acceptance, when one sends back the contract with a signature, which is sent from the partner with his signature.

In other cases, if the concluded document is not completed at the stage of agreement of special terms and conditions, the contract would be made and exchanged immediately. In this case, the agreement is made through negotiation. A contract is a confirmation of agreement. Therefore, it is considered that the contract and the approval of contract are not related nor is it considered necessary.

It is a fact that an agreement can be approved without a contract. Proforma invoice is used instead of an official contract. However, it may become a cause of an argument and it takes more time to solve the problem in court if there is no contract. Moreover, it is necessary to hand in the contract when applying for an export license or export loan. At this point, a contract has to be made and exchanged in advance.

There are various items shown on the title page of a contract. The sales contract, the purchase contract, the sale note and the purchase note are the most common. However, no matter what kind of title page is used, the most important thing is that sufficient terms and conditions are written on it for carrying out a contract.

Two copies of a contract with signatures are to be made. Then, both copies with signatures are sent to the transaction partner. The partner is asked to send one copy back so that both transaction partners have the same contract.

The signature is signed by the person who has the right. It is considered that the head of a department has a limited right to sign. If it is a small business transaction, the signature of the person who is in charge is recognized. However, the minutes or power of attorney of executive meetings might be necessary for transaction involving a large amount of money or in long term transaction.

On the face of the contract, the agreement of the specific terms and conditions are written. On the back, the general terms and conditions are written. If the general terms and conditions are not agreed upon, the specific terms and conditions must be agreed upon, using the contract form of one's own company. If a partner sends his own company's contract form in advance; read through the face and the back page of the contract. Any conditions that cannot be agreed must be deleted and sent back.

2 Content of Specific Terms and Conditions

2-1 Quality
A decision is made here on what kinds of goods should be dealt with. In addition to the name of the goods, the item number, the model number or color are factors used to make a decision. In Format 3, the item number, name of goods and model number are written under description to identify the quality of goods.

In principle, the quality of the sample has to be the same as the actual goods if a sample is used to decide the quality of goods in negotiation. When the actual goods and the sample differ slightly, the article "The Goods are not necessarily the same in quality as the sample" should be written in the section OTHER TERMS AND CONDITIONS on the contract.

Format 3: Specific Terms and Conditions

KURUME SHINKO CO., INC
3-4-5 Higashimachi, Kurume
Fukuoka 830-0011 JAPAN

SALES CONTRACT

Date: Dec. 27, 2000
Buyer: Protrade, P8G3 Thuang An District,
   Binh Duang Province, Vietnam

DESCRIPTION	QUANTITY	UNIT PRICE	AMOUNT
SHINKO BOND E-20210	20KGS X 600 CARTONS	JP¥120 PER KIRO. CIF HOCHIMINH	JP¥1,440,000

TOTAL JP¥1,440,000

Payment Terms: DOCUMENTARY DRAFT AT SIGHT UNDER IRREVOCABLE L/C
Insurance: AGAINST ALL RISKS INCLUDING WAR & S.R.C.C. RISKS FOR 110% OF INVOICE VALUE
Delivery: JANUARY, 2001
Packing: USUAL PACKING FOR CONTAINER
Inspection:
Other Terms and Conditions:

(Buyer)   (Seller)

by _____   by _____

Please sign and return the duplicate immediately.

The quality of the goods could not be consistent. Some may be in bad conditions. In that case, an allowance of an inferior grade product is decided. In OTHER TERMS AND CONDITION, after indicating the allowance, the agreed pieces or percentage of the inferior quality products are written. After the allowance is decided, the actual amount of payment of the mixed goods should also be decided then.

2-2   Quantity

The measurement of quantity is classified into weight, measurement, piece, unit dozen, package, set, length, and square depending on the various goods.

We have to pay attention to how ton is used for measurement. The three types of measurements used across the world are long ton, short ton, and metric ton so it is important to know the differences between them. Moreover, when calculating the Sea freight, we use measurement ton. We have to be careful not to make a mistake.

The number of pieces that is in one package has to be clearly shown at the beginning of transaction in order to express the amount of package and to avoid arguments.

The More or Less Clause must be settled in cases where the amounts may differ, as in agricultural produce and natural resources. "5% more or less" is written after the amount, for instance. For goods that are recognized as More or Less products, payment varies depending on the actual number of goods; therefore, "about, approximately or circa" should be indicated before the price.

2-3   Price

If the division of costs is not decided between the buyer and the seller, the price cannot be calculated; therefore, trade terms have to be agreed upon first. Similarly, the currency of price that has been chosen should also be shown. The price shows the unit price and the total amount of the product.

After trade terms have come to an agreement, the price has to be decided. The trade terms have to be indicated after the price as in this example, "US$398.00 CIP Auckland".

The shown currency of price can be anything as long as it is agreed upon. However, international transaction cannot be done if the currency is not circulated world widely. In actual practice, the US$, Euro, Yen, and Pound are used commonly. For example, there are many countries that use the same currency as the US dollar and Pound (British). Therefore, the name of the country must be shown after US$ or UK Pound.

The indicated price has to be very definite without any mistakes. Then, the unit price and amount have to be written in the contract. Moreover, if it is predicted that low quality products are mixed in the same consignment, "about, approximately, circa" etc. must be indicated before the price.

2-4 Payment

First of all, we have to decide how to make a payment. If a bill of exchange is used, its term must be decided as well.

In the method of payment, there are advance payment and deferred Payment. Deferred payment includes open account, documentary letter of credit and documentary collection.

Advance payment is a method in which the buyer pays for the goods before they are dispatched. This is used when the buyer's credibility is unknown and is unable to obtain a letter of credit. This is also used as a matter of convenience for small orders. The payment is made by sending remittance from the import bank to the export bank. The two kinds of remittance are mail transfer and telegraphic transfer. For advance payment, "Advance payment by mail transfer within 15 days after contract" is written in the contract, for instance.

Figure 5   Payment Method

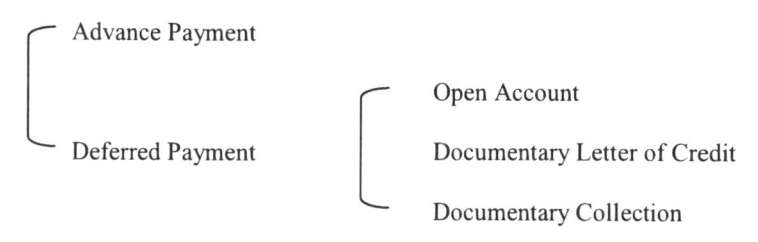

- Advance Payment
- Deferred Payment

- Open Account
- Documentary Letter of Credit
- Documentary Collection

An open account is the means of payment in which the seller extends the credit directly to the buyer. The exporter delivers the goods and the importer remit to the exporter's bank account directly. In particular, the exporter delivers the cargo, makes and sends shipping documents to the importer. The shipping documents usually consist of a commercial invoice, a transport document, an insurance policy and so on. The importer remits to the exporter's account by telegraphic transfer within the stipulated period. The seller thus takes direct risk for the buyer's insolvency or unwillingness to pay. In international commerce, a long-standing relationship usually exists between the buyer and seller. For example, "Open account payment within 30 days after shipping date" is written in the contract.

Next is the documentary letter of credit. A letter of credit, also referred to as an L/C, is a document issued by a financial institution which acts as an irrevocable guarantee of payment to a beneficiary. This means that the bank pays if the applicant obtaining the L/C fails to perform its obligations. The L/C can also be the source of payment for a transaction, meaning that an exporter will get paid by redeeming the letter of credit. Today, letters of credit are used almost exclusively in international trade transactions of significant value, for deals between a supplier in one country and a wholesale customer in another. The parties to a letter of credit are usually an applicant who wants to send money, a beneficiary who is to receive the money, the issuing bank of whom the applicant is a client, and the advising bank of whom the beneficiary is a client.

Figure 6 Flow of documentary letter of credit payment

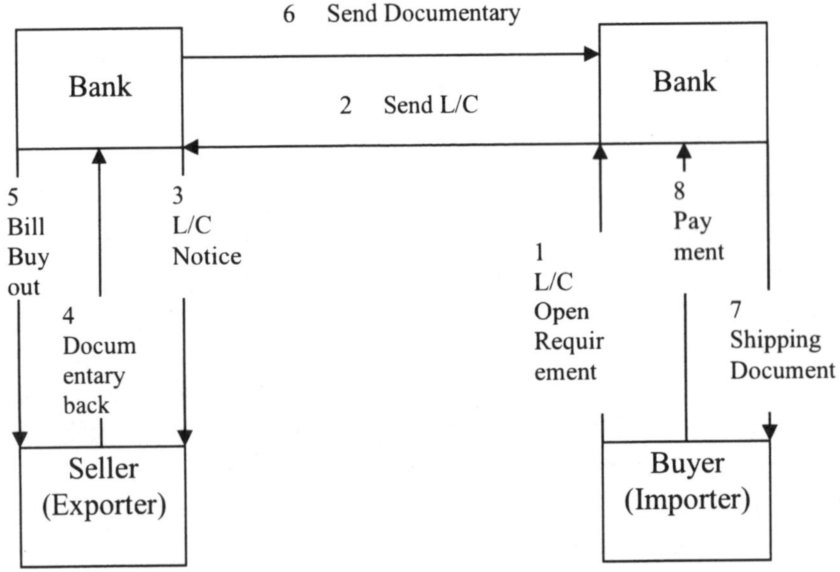

```
                    6   Send Documentary
    ┌─────────┐ ───────────────────────────→ ┌─────────┐
    │  Bank   │                              │  Bank   │
    │         │ ←─────── 2  Send L/C ─────── │         │
    └─────────┘                              └─────────┘
      ↑   │                                    ↑    │
      │   │                                    │    │
   5  │   │ 3                               1  │    │ 8
   Bill   │ L/C                             L/C│    Pay
   Buy    │ Notice                          Open│   ment
   out    │                                 Requir    │
          │ 4                               ement     │ 7
          │ Docum                                     │ Shipping
          │ entary                                    │ Document
          │ back                                      │
          ↓   ↓                                    ↓   ↓
    ┌─────────┐                              ┌─────────┐
    │  Seller │                              │  Buyer  │
    │(Exporter)│                             │(Importer)│
    └─────────┘                              └─────────┘
```

In some occasions a supplier may require a company or an individual to provide a guarantee of payment. This usually occurs when a considerable sum of money is involved; for instance, for the purchase of a car, a home, for stock or plant equipment for a business.

In this case a documentary letter of credit provides the necessary guarantee and can be obtained by the company's or individual's bank. This letter guarantees payment to the supplier on condition that the correct documents (specified in the banks terms and conditions outlined as an accompaniment to the letter of credit) are presented.

A letter of credit is often used for transacting with suppliers not easily accessible to the buyer; sourcing products from an overseas

Chapter 3 Specific Terms and Conditions 57

supplier and contains the terms of the contract. These terms must be complied with, prior to the bank releasing payment to the supplier. This may include delivery time, quality, payment terms, and an independent third party testing the goods. If a supplier accepts the letter of credit, then the bank will supply and comply with their part of the agreement. The bank then recoups payment from the individual or the company seeking the line of credit in the first place.

A letter of credit usually places the buyer in a position of greater bargaining power in their trade negotiations when compared to using alternative means of payment. This is because they already have and can show the surety of payment as a part of the negotiation process.

A draft or bill of exchange is a negotiable instrument that is payable to the seller and drawn on the issuing bank and/or the buyer. This document is prepared by the seller, but is analogous to a check written by the buyer to the seller. Drafts can be either "sight drafts" where the bank pays the full amount of the draft upon the seller's presentation, or "time drafts" where the bank's obligation at the time of presentation is merely to accept the draft for payment at a later date (e.g. 90 days after the seller's presentation). Time drafts provide the buyer with short-term financing. Often, banks will purchase their accepted time drafts at a discounted rate.

A documentary letter of credit is used in the sample specific terms and the "Documentary Draft at Sight under Irrevocable L/C" is used for the conditions in Format 3.

In banking practice, a documentary collection is used in the buyer's and seller's country for the seller to present commercial documents (e.g., invoices) to the buyer along with a payment demand (usually a bill of exchange). There are two types of documentary collections: the D/P (Documents against Payment) and D/A (Documents against Acceptance). D/P is the documents surrendered [by the bank] to the importer/buyer after the importer/buyer has accepted the accompanying draft, acknowledging the obligation to pay at a later date. D/A is a sight draft to which the title documents are attached. The documents are surrendered to the importer/buyer after he/she has paid the accompanying draft. For instance, "Draft at Sight under D/P" or "Draft at 30 d/s under D/A" is stipulated in the contract for documentary collection.

Figure 7   Flow of documentary collection payment

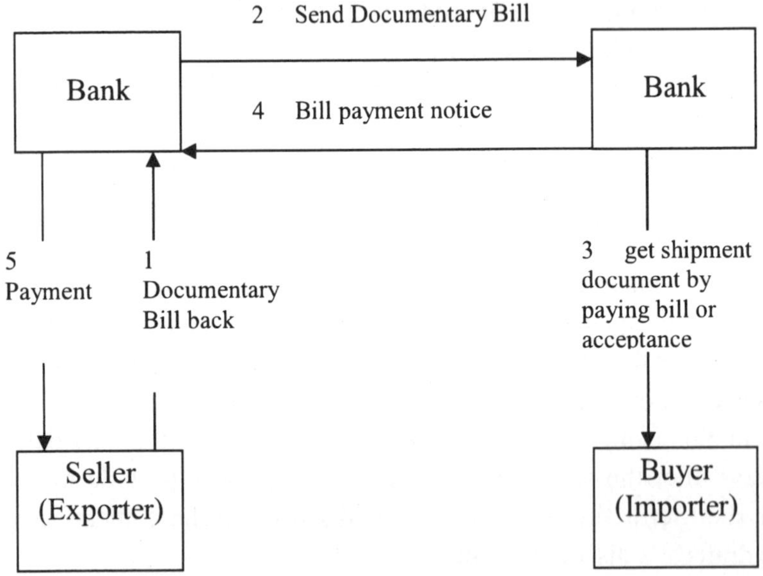

```
                    2  Send Documentary Bill
    ┌──────────┐ ─────────────────────────→ ┌──────────┐
    │   Bank   │                            │   Bank   │
    │          │ ←───────────────────────── │          │
    └──────────┘    4  Bill payment notice  └──────────┘
         │  ▲                                    │
         │  │                                    │
    5    │  │ 1                          3  get shipment
  Payment│  │ Documentary                   document by
         │  │ Bill back                     paying bill or
         │  │                               acceptance
         ▼  │                                    ▼
    ┌──────────┐                            ┌──────────┐
    │  Seller  │                            │  Buyer   │
    │(Exporter)│                            │(Importer)│
    └──────────┘                            └──────────┘
```

Open account and D/A share the same characteristics. The buyer can get the documents immediately and the payment is predicted to be in a certain time period. These two types of payment are called supplier's credit.

2-5   Cargo Insurance

Cargo Insurance is an insurance protecting cargo being transported by a carrier. In trade terms, the seller has to have all cargo insured in case of CIF and CIP. Insurance terms and conditions, risks and insurance amounts need to be discussed in cargo insurance. There are three types of cargo insurance: Free from Particular Average (FPA), With Average (WA), and All Risks.

The three types are the conditions of the old policy. In 1982, the Institute of London Underwriters made a new policy. Now, both old and new policies are used together. The terms of the new policy are based on those of the old policy. The terms of the old policy are FPA, WA and All Risks: the counterparts of the new one are ICC (Institute Cargo Clause) (A) (B) (C). These terms will be explained in detail later.

For air cargo, there is the shipper's interest for small cargo and the insurance on Institute Air Cargo Clauses. The terms available are only All Risks or ICC (A).

In Free from Particular Average (FPA) and With Average (WA), the insurance company which is responsible for the risk is restricted. Even if All Risks are adopted, it is not secured if the risks of war and strikes are not specified as an additional contract. Therefore, the extraneous risks are to be decided in an additional insurance. The conditions that are seen often actually are All Risks with War & S.R.C.C. as extraneous risks.

The next issue is the insured amount. The insured amount is the amount which is agreed on in the contract. It is the maximum amount that the insurance company pays when the cargo is damaged. However, the insured amount is calculated as CIF + 10% (Imaginary Profit for the importer), so the seller and buyer do not decide on the amount by themselves.

In Format 3, "Against All Risks including War & S.R.C.C. for 110% of Invoice Value" is specified. S.R.C.C. means "Strike, Riots and Civil Commotions." They are classified as Strike Risks. "Invoice Value" is the amount of invoice, but this contract is under CIF and the Invoice Value means the CIF amount.

Under the principle of CIF and CIP in Incoterms, the minimum insurance terms are FPA, or the ICC (C). It is a requirement to have this insurance. In case of specifying additional terms and conditions or risks, the buyer has to bear the additional insurance fee. However, in practice, the seller bears most of the cost.

2-6 Delivery

There is a time limit for delivery from the seller to the buyer. The time of delivery or the deadline of delivery must be decided. There are three appointed methods for the time of delivery: by date, by week, and by month.

In the method of appointing a date, the specified day, such as "November 8" is determined. For appointing a week, the number of week, such as "3rd Week of August" is decided. For appointing a month, "September Delivery" or "September to October Delivery" is the way to show the appointed time of delivery. For "September Delivery", the delivery has to be made within September 1st to September 30th. Likewise, "September to October Delivery" means sometime from September 1st to October 31st. If there is a delay in delivery, it becomes a violation of contract.

There is also another way to show the time of delivery as "Within 50 days after contract" or "Within 30 days after receipt of L/C".

When the goods are in stock, and the delivery can be made immediately, it is called "Immediate Shipment". However, we should avoid Immediate Shipment because the definite date or other conditions are not clear.

In practice, "Shipment" is regarded as synonymous with delivery. That is because FOB, C&F and CIF are the most common terms where shipment is the time of delivery. However, as in container ship or air craft, the time of shipment and delivery are not the same, so we should understand the difference between them.

Questions

1 Explain the significance of firm offer.
2 Explain briefly each item of the special terms and conditions.
3 In special terms and conditions, units of days, weeks and months are used for delivery. How and in what circumstances are these units used? Discuss this in class from the perspectives of the types of goods and their quality, the distance of the export and import country and the means of transport.
4 Discuss in class the strong and weak points of open account payment, document letter of credit, and document collection.

Part 2 Contract Fulfillment Preparation

Chapter 1
Obtaining License of Export and Import

Summary

After signing the contract, preparation should be made for contract fulfillment. The first thing is to obtain an export and import license from the government if necessary. Other certificates such as PSI, Certificate of Origin and Fumigation Certificate that are issued by the export country and are to be handed over to import customs can also be obtained at this stage if necessary. More over, an Inspection Certificate for demonstrating the quality should also be obtained if necessary.

1   Export and Import License

1-1   Trade Control Institution

In Japan, Foreign Exchange and Foreign Trade Law is the basic law for trade control. In real practice, it is controlled by government ordinances such as export ordinance, import ordinance and exchange ordinance. Export and import customs entry is controlled by the customs law, tariff rate law, and tariff temporary measures law. Not only these laws, but inspection law and export-import transaction law also regulate trade transaction. The two regulations will not to be explained here, however, since no item is related to the quality inspection law and only the pearl is regulated by the latter one.

    Moreover, there are times when trade items are regulated by domestic regulations. For example, when importing or exporting some 30 items of goods which are regulated by "Plant Epidemic Prevention Law", "Animal Infection Prevention Law", "Export and Import Transaction Law" and "Food Sanitation Law", certificates or inspection approval should be obtained following a specified procedure from the related ministries. The items should be handed at Customs when going through. These items will not be introduced here, although, it is better to confirm what kinds of items are regulated before trading.

Furthermore, when exporting from Japan, certificates and inspection approvals issued by Japan should be submitted when going through import customs according to laws of the destination countries. If required by the importer, certificates such as PSI and Certificate of Quarantine should be obtained.

In this chapter, export and import licenses will be explained following export ordinance and import ordinance. Both export and import are based on the principle of freedom. Yet, in the case of special items, export permission and export approval might become necessary when exporting, and import quota and import approval when importing. Such licenses are issued by the Minister of Economy and Industry.

1-2　Export License
The items that need export license are listed in "Export Ordinance". Export license is parted into export permission and export approval. The objective of the former one is to maintain international peace and security and the objective of the latter one is to balance international support and the healthy development of trade and domestic economy. As shown in Figure 8, export permission has list control and catch-all control.

The list control refers to the items listed by "Export Ordinance", which are also called strategic items, including items such as weapons, chemical weapon related equipment, missile related equipment, and so forth. Items of the Wassenaar Arrangement are also included. The Wassenaar Arrangement is a treaty concluded in 1996 for controlling the international transaction of strategy supply.

Figure 8   Content of export and import licenses

- Export Permission
  - List control items
  - Catch-all control items
- Export Approval
  - Domestic demand & supply adjustment supply
  - Export order maintenance supply
  - International agreement supply
  - UN economic sanction supply
  - Consignment processing trade supply
  - Export prohibited supply

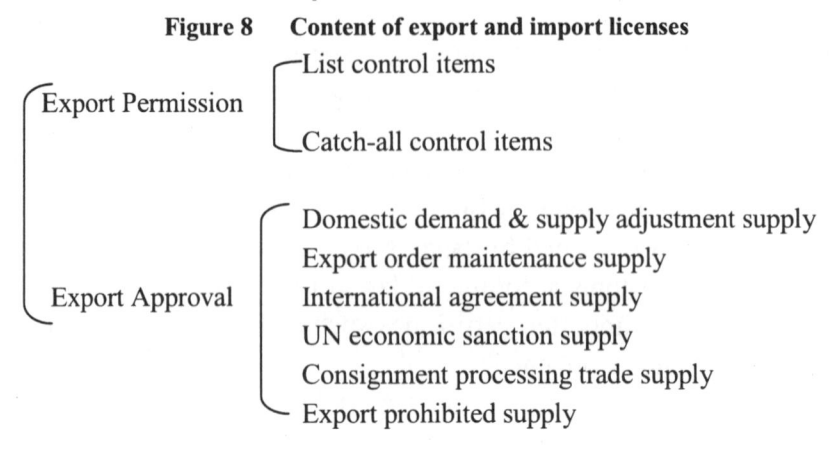

Besides the items listed, export permission should be obtained for all items except for some furniture, wood, cloths, and food under certain conditions. Since this regulation regulates almost all kinds of goods, it is named Catch-all control. The conditions are that the Ministry of Economy and Industry gives notification to exporters about the items that can be used for the development of weapons of mass destructions or if there is a possibility. However, if the export partner is in the U.S., Canada and EU countries, this Catch-all control is not applied.

There are six cases when export approval is necessary as shown in Figure 8. Items for domestic demand and supply adjustment are regulated from the view of maintaining Japan domestic supply quantity. Items for export order maintenance refer to items regulated in order to keep the economic order of the import place. International agreement items refer to the items regulated on commercial transaction by international treaties. At present, endangered plants and animals regulated by the Washington Convention, special poisonous wastes regulated by the Basel Treaty and ozone destructive material regulated by the Montreal Protocol are objects that are regulated. UN economic sanction items refer to the overall transaction regulation on the nations and regions sanctioned by the UN economic sanction. There are also times when only a part of the specific items are regulated. Consignment processing trade supply refers to the regulation of raw material for foreign consignment processing. At present, the export of leather and cotton or silk for squeeze processing should obtain export approval. Contraband items refer to the items that are prohibited from exporting such as national treasures, drugs, fake currencies and so on.

1-3 Obtaining Export License

When traders are requested by law to obtain an exporting license, they must apply to the Ministry of Economy and Industry which has the authority to issue export permission and export approval. If other certificates are necessary, application should be made to the related Ministries. After obtaining export permission and approval certificates, they need to be submitted at customs for clearance.

Figure 9   Flow of export license obtainment

```
┌──────────────┐     ┌──────────────────────────┐
│ Regulations  │───▶ │ Export permission from   │
│ by trade     │     │ the Minister of Economy  │
│ related laws │     │ and Industry             │────┐
└──────────────┘  │  └──────────────────────────┘    │
                  │  ┌──────────────────────────┐    │
                  └─▶│ Export approval from the │    │   ┌──────────────┐
                     │ Minister of Economy and  │    │──▶│ Export       │
                     │ Industry                 │────│   │ customs      │
                     └──────────────────────────┘    │   │ entry        │
┌──────────────┐                                     │   └──────────────┘
│ Regulations  │                                     │
│ by nation    │───▶ ┌──────────────────────────┐    │
│ related laws │     │ Certificates from        │────┘
└──────────────┘     │ related Ministers        │
                     └──────────────────────────┘
```

Applications should be made when the contract has been concluded. In practice, a copy of the contract must also be submitted. Yet, an export license cannot always be obtained. For this reason, when regulated goods are to be exported, the contract should be signed based on "subject to export license"; if the license is not obtained, the contract itself becomes invalid.

1-4 Obtaining Import License

Figure 10 is used for discussing import license. First of all, some items such as publications which violate intellectual rights, fake currencies, pistols and drugs are prohibited from being imported. They are called contraband items.

In the regulation on import, there are regulations made by trade related laws and others by domestic laws. Regulation of trade related laws are different from those of export. Import publication and import announcement are applied to import restriction. Import publication, which is made regularly by the official gazette and Economy Industry Ministry gazette, should always be referred to in order to confirm import regulated items. Import publication keeps a list of import quota items, a list of shipment area and origin place for items that need import approval, and a list for items that need confirmation.

For import quota items, an announcement will be made on the import quota application for each item or group of items. This is called an import announcement. Import announcements are also made regularly by the official gazette and the Economy Industry Ministry gazette. When importing import quota goods, the import quota should be obtained from the Ministry of Economy and Industry. For some items, an import approval should also be obtained at this time. For the rest of the items, import approvals must be obtained after receiving the import quota.

The second list in import publications contains the items from countries, shipment area or region that requires import approval. When importing such items, import approval should be applied for with the Ministry of Economy and Industry.

The third list shows "confirmation" items that do not require import approval, but should be controlled from the perspectives of domestic laws or international treaties. In import publications, items which require the related Ministry's confirmation and customs clearance confirmation are listed.

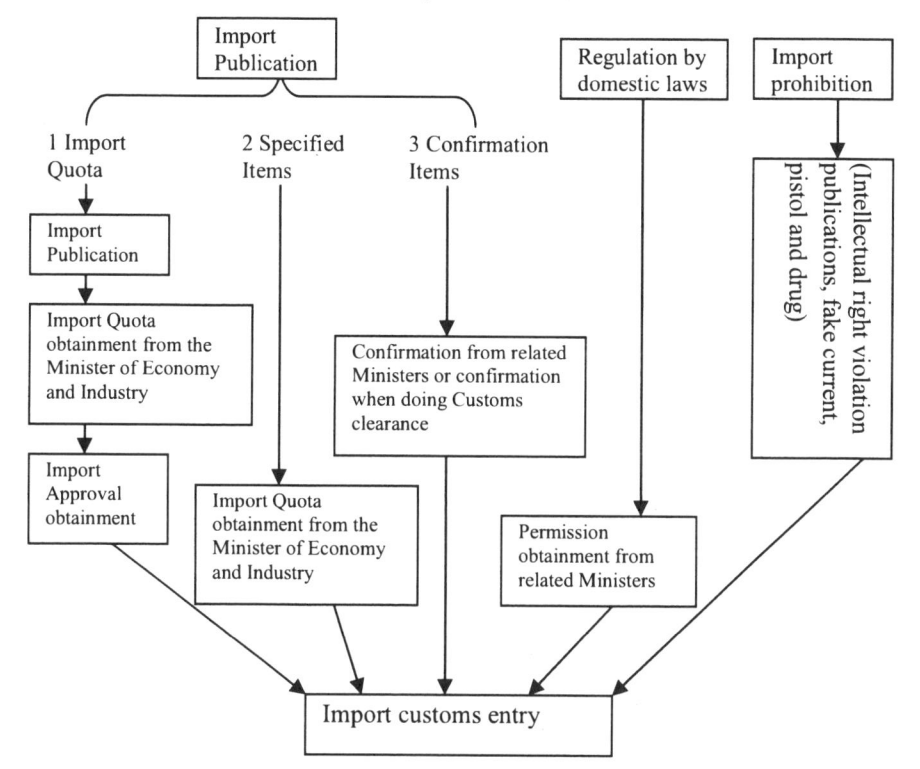

Chapter 1 Obtaining License of Export and Import 69

Figure 10   Content of import license and flow of obtainment

```
                    ┌──────────────┐         ┌──────────────┐    ┌──────────────┐
                    │   Import     │         │ Regulation by│    │   Import     │
                    │  Publication │         │ domestic laws│    │  prohibition │
                    └──────────────┘         └──────────────┘    └──────────────┘
              ┌───────────┼───────────┐                                  │
              ▼           ▼           ▼                                  ▼
         1 Import    2 Specified  3 Confirmation                  (Intellectual right
          Quota        Items        Items                          violation publications,
            │            │            │                            fake current,
            ▼            │            │                            pistol and drug)
       ┌─────────┐       │            │
       │ Import  │       │            │
       │Publication│     │            │
       └─────────┘       │            │
            │            │            ▼
            ▼            │    ┌──────────────────┐
    ┌──────────────┐     │    │ Confirmation from│
    │ Import Quota │     │    │ related Ministers│
    │obtainment from│    │    │ or confirmation  │
    │the Minister of│    │    │ when doing Customs│
    │Economy and   │     │    │ clearance        │
    │Industry      │     │    └──────────────────┘
    └──────────────┘     │            │
            │            ▼            │
            ▼    ┌──────────────┐     │    ┌──────────────┐
    ┌──────────┐ │ Import Quota │     │    │  Permission  │
    │  Import  │ │obtainment from│    │    │obtainment from│
    │ Approval │ │the Minister of│    │    │related Ministers│
    │obtainment│ │Economy and   │     │    └──────────────┘
    └──────────┘ │Industry      │     │            │
         │       └──────────────┘     │            │
         │              │             │            │
         └──────────────┴─────────────┴────────────┴──────┐
                                                          ▼
                           ┌──────────────────────────────────┐
                           │     Import customs entry         │
                           └──────────────────────────────────┘
```

In addition to the above items that are regulated by trade related laws, there are also items regulated by domestic laws. For example, food and some kinds of toys are objects of "Food Sanitation Law" and necessary documents should be submitted to the Ministry of Health Welfare and Labor Quarantine Office. Before importing, items should be checked whether they are regulated by some laws. The customs will check if you have applied. If the items are regulated, permission should be obtained from the Ministers of related ministries.

There are occasions when a sales contract is needed when applying for an import license. Here, the agreement "subject to import license" is necessary if the contract is to be signed.

2 Obtaining Other Certificates

If required by the importer, certificates such as PSI, Certificate of Origin and Fumigation Certificate should be arranged. In Incoterms, the importer should pay for such certificates that are issued in the export country and used in import customs entry. The Inspection certificate and quality certificate should be obtained at the time if mentioned in the contract.

In PSI (Pre-Shipment Inspection), the quality and cost of goods are inspected before shipment and the appropriate price is determined. This is done to prevent declarations of false pricing for tariff evasion and dumping. In Japan, PSI is required when exporting used machinery to Asia, Africa and Middle-eastern countries. In this occasion, the exporter should obtain a certificate from a maritime inspection office and deliver it to the importer. The Certificate of Origin is a certificate proving that the item originated or was produced in a specific area or country. It is used for import control. The main objective of this regulation is the application of preferential duties and import restriction on goods of certain countries. The Certificate of Origin is usually issued by the Chamber of Commerce and Industry. However, when applying for preferential duties, the certificate of "Form A" should be used.

Wood itself is rarely exported from Japan to other countries, but it is used in packing and piling cargo. In this case, fumigation will be required by the import country for bugging. The exporter should then ask an inspection company for fumigation; obtain a Fumigation Certificate and deliver it to the importer. On the contrary, when importing to Japan, various kinds of certificates such as the Certificate of Quarantine for animals and plants are required. Necessary certificates should be mentioned in the contract or L/C.

There are times when the importer requires documents demonstrating that the goods imported match the one written in the contract. Such documents are known as the Inspection Certificate and the Certificate of Quality Inspection. Inspection can be carried out by special inspection companies or can be carried out by the exporter or manufacturer themselves. Whatever the measure is, inspection organizations should be mentioned in the contract under such conditions.

Sale by Standard is a common practice when importing natural resources and agricultural products as mentioned in Chapter 2. Some examples are the USG, which sets the standard made by public organizations; GMQ, which is used for wood and frozen fish; FAQ, which is used to show the annual average quality of grain, and so on. To set the standard for transaction goods, the Certificate of Quality Inspection issued by public organizations is often required. Under such conditions, the inspection organizations should also be mentioned in the contract.

Questions

1 Explain about the export license.
2 Explain about the import quota institution.
3 Discuss the background of Catch-all control in class.

Chapter 2
Logistics Arrangement

Summary

Originally in wartime, logistics meant military support and the shipment of supplies to the front row; however, in mass production, it means supplying strategic integrated supplies of production, distribution and sales. The implication here is the rational movement of cargo. An exporter would arrange the freight shipment and actually would ask a forwarder to do the necessary things. In the case of the importer, he would also request a forwarder to arrange for the necessary procedure and transportation from the import port to the warehouse of the importer. Here we will study methods and related documents of international transport.

1 Requesting Forwarders

The exporter would prepare freight shipment and the importer prepare for receiving the freight. For both sides, making arrangements with the forwarder is the main business.

A forwarder is the person who is responsible for the overall distribution process of freight in the export and import place. He is qualified as a customs clearance agent, possesses domestic means of transportation such as trucks, and is also qualified as a sea trader who does a series of work such as freight loading and unloading in harbors. Moreover, he can also act as an agent for shipping, airline and even an insurance company. Although the process of freight distribution is very complicated, it can be said that rational distribution is made possible because of the existence of the forwarder.

The exporter would ask the forwarder to do a series of work and help with the procedure of shipping the freight. The requirements vary by trade terms in the sales contracts. In EXW, it is not necessary for the exporter to ask for forwarders. In FOB, cargo insurance and arrangement of international transport not necessary for the exporter, either. In C&F, not only would international transport be required for but cargo insurance as well. The conditions would be opposite for the importer. In fact, the division of cost for the exporter and importer is determined based on the selected trade terms; the forwarder would be asked to carry out the procedures and each cost burden.

The exporter and the importer would ask the forwarder to carry out the procedures mentioned above. Here we will discuss the traditional terms of FOB, C&F and CIF.

The exporter would make the necessary shipping instructions and commercial invoice and hand them over to the forwarder. Shipping instructions are the documents about shipping and customs clearance. The format is not set, but is written in the exporter or the forwarder's style. The shipping instructions must have no errors since the document necessary for shipping and the customs clearance that forwarder make is based on it.

The commercial invoice is a shipment guidebook and a bill as well. This document is not formatted and would be written in the exporter's own style. However, crucial contents must be included as it is used for export import customs entry. Detailed contents are regulated by the tariff law enforcement.

The exporter would make the packing list. The exporter may ask the forwarder to make this list. This supplements the commercial invoice and provides details about product packing. Exporters do not need to make these documents. Although they have to submit the commercial invoice at the customs clearance, exporters can send it directly or through its bank.

The series of work and the procedure of distribution by the

forwarder have been discussed above. However, international transport and cargo insurance come to a conclusion in the shipping and insurance contracts through the forwarders who act as agents of shipping, airline and even insurance companies. Therefore, exporters and importers should not leave everything to the forwarder, but need to have essential knowledge as well. Cargo insurance will be discussed in the next chapter. In this chapter, we will learn the basics of international transport.

2   Types of International Transport

When using the trade terms of FOB, the importers would arrange international transportation; in terms of C&F and CIP, the exporters would be responsible for that instead. In Japan which is surrounded by sea, all transport means, maritime transport, air transport, and combined transport are applied.

In maritime transport, a liner is used to transport a lot of cargo of the shippers together or a specific shipper transports the cargo of a charter party. Most of the liners are container ships, and in charter bulk ships and tankers are used.

Now we will try to categorize the liner in container transport by the cargo quantity. If a container is full, the cargo would be called Full Container Load Cargo (FCL); if not full, it would be called Less Than Container Load Cargo (LCL). Even if it does not fill up a container, it is called FCL if it uses one container to transport. FCL cargo would be pilled up in the container then brought to Container Yard; thus it can be called Container Yard Cargo or CY cargo as well.

A shipping company or forwarders would be asked to ship cargo that does not fill up a container. In the case of asking the shipping company directly, the cargo would be brought to the Container Freight Station inside the Container Yard. A shipping company would pack the cargo together into one container; thus the cargo would be

Format 4: Shipping Instructions

SHIPPING INSTRUCTION

Shipper	山九株式会社
KURUME SHINKO CO. INC 3-4-5 HIGASHI-MACHI, KURUME FUKUOKA, 830-0011, JAPAN	物流営業部 九州営業グループ 〒812-0011 福岡市博多区博多駅前 2丁目20番1号 大博多ビル8F TEL　092(431)4439（代表）
Consignee　PROTRADE P8G3 THUAN AN DISTRCT BINH DUONG PROVINCE VIETNAM TEL:086-65-85594	FAX　092(451)3439 （担当　　　　）　　課　　　係 電話
Nortify party	Invoice No. K-010117　　Date: JAN. 17, 2001
SAME AS CONSIGNEE	Booking No. [x] コンテナー船積　　[ ] 在来船積 [x] CY-CY　　[ ] CY-CFS [ ] CFS-CY　　[ ] CFS-CFS
	From/Place of receipt NAGOYA CY	CY/CFS 締切日時　　通関締切日
Ocean Vessel WAN HAI 165	Port of loading NAGOYA, JAPAN	Arrival & Sailing Date FEB. 9-10, 2001
Port of discharge HOCHIMINH CITY, VIETNAM	For transhipment to/Place of delivery HOCHIMINH CITY CY	Final destination (for the shipper's reference only)
Marks and Numbers	No. of pkgs.	Description of goods
N/M	10 PALLETS (600 CARTONS)	SHINKO BOND E-20210 20 KGS X 600 CARTONS G/W:12,820 KGS 24.188 M3

上記事項は必ずB／LのDESCRIPTION欄に記載います。

Freight & Charge	Freight: PREPAID	
US$550.00(WAN HAI LINES)	B/L発行地: NAGOYA, JAPAN	B/L Date: SAILING DATE

必要書類	B/L		W/M List	INS POLICY	E/D Loaded			備考 海上貨物保険を付保願います。
	Org.	Copy						WAN HAI LINES
	3			2				06-4963-8601
添付書	L/C		INV.	P/L	検査証	E/L	成分表	矢部様へBOOKING願います。
	Org.	Copy						
			3	3			1	
Maker大鹿振興(株)	Cargo搬入先：名港海運(株)	Cargo搬入月日：	2月5日

Format 5: Commercial Invoice

INVOICE

KURUME SHINKO CO. INC
3-4-5 HIGASHI-MACHI, KURUME
FUKUOKA, 830-0011, JAPAN

DATE: JAN.17,2001

MESSRS. PROTRADE, THE UNION OF MANUFACTORIES PRODUCING AND TRADING GOODS
ADDRESS. THUAN AN DISTRICT BINH DUONG PROVINCE, VIETNAM
ATTN: MR. YOSHIHARA
TEL 084-65-855914

INVOICE NO. K-010117
CONTRACT NO.
L/C NO. 8710

PORT OF SHIPMENT: NAGOYA, JAPAN
PORT OF DESTINATION: HOCHIMINH, VIETNAM
VIA:
DATE OF SHIPEMNT: FEB.10, 2001
VESSEL: WAN HAI 165
TERMS: CIF HOCHIMINH

MARKS & NOS.	DESCRIPTION	QUANTITY KG	PRICE PER KG	AMOUNT
N/M	SHINKO BOND E-20210 20KGS x 600 CARTONS	12,000	120	CIF HOCHIMINH CITY 1,440,000
	TOTAL: 600 CARTONS	12,000 KGS		JPY1,440,000.-

KURUME SHINKO CO. INC

Format 6: Packing List

PACKING LIST

KURUME SHINKO CO. INC
3-4-5 HIGASHI-MACHI, KURUME
FUKUOKA, 830-0011, JAPAN

MESSRS.	PROTRADE		INVOICE NO.	DATE
ADDRESS.	P8G3 THUAN AN DISTRCT BINH DUONG PROVINCE VIETNAM TEL:086-65-85594		K-010117	JAN.17,2001
			L/C NO.	

PORT OF SHIPMENT	PORT OF DESTINATION	VIA
NAGOYA, JAPAN	HOCHIMINH CITY, VIETNAM	
DATE OF SHIPEMNT	VESSEL	
FEB.10,2001	WAN HAI 165	

MARKS & NOS.	DESCRIPTION	QUANTITY	WEIGHT NET	WEIGHT GROSS	MEASUREMENT
		KG	KG	KG	L x W x H (CM M3
N/M	SHINKO BOND E-20210				
	A-TYPE PALLET 20KG x 60 CARTONS x 5 PALLETS	6,000	6,000	6,410	125x100x188 11.750 M3
	B-TYPE PALLET 20KG x 60 CARTONS x 5 PALLETS	6,000	6,000	6,410	100x125x199 12.438 M3
	TOTAL: 10 PALLETS (600 CARTONS)		12,000	12,820	24.188 M3
	OSHIKA SHINKO CO., LTD.				

called Container Freight Station Cargo and CF freight. In the case of forwarders, a consolidator, not related to the shipping company, would be asked to transport small cargo. The forwarders would pack the combined cargo into containers, which are then taken to different destinations in their company trucks, and brought straightly to the Container Yard.

Air transport can be divided into Direct Cargo and Consolidated Cargo. Direct Cargo would be shipped by transportation companies, which are contracted as Air Cargo Agents.

Figure 11   Types of international transport

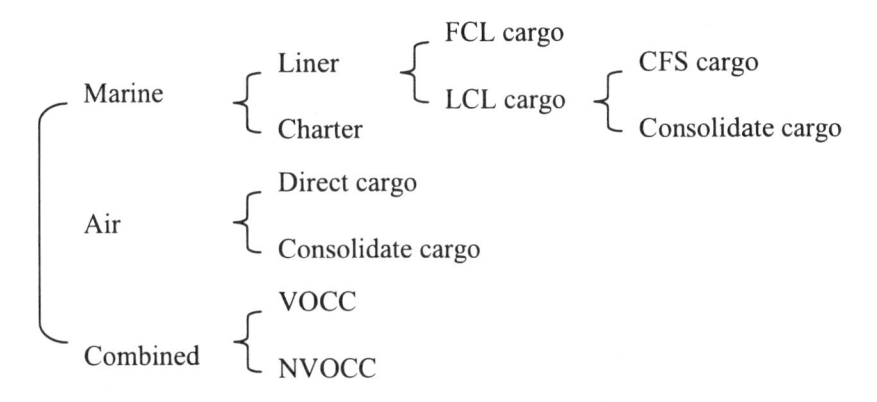

$$
\left\{
\begin{array}{l}
\text{Marine} \left\{ \begin{array}{l} \text{Liner} \left\{ \begin{array}{l} \text{FCL cargo} \\ \text{LCL cargo} \end{array} \right. \left\{ \begin{array}{l} \text{CFS cargo} \\ \text{Consolidate cargo} \end{array} \right. \\ \text{Charter} \end{array} \right. \\
\text{Air} \left\{ \begin{array}{l} \text{Direct cargo} \\ \text{Consolidate cargo} \end{array} \right. \\
\text{Combined} \left\{ \begin{array}{l} \text{VOCC} \\ \text{NVOCC} \end{array} \right.
\end{array}
\right.
$$

Consolidated cargo would be contracted with the forwarders, who would pack the cargo together with others into containers to be taken to different destinations and ask the shipping companies for shipment.

In addition to maritime and airline transport, there is Multi-modal (combined) transport. Because it combines various means of transport for shipment, it can issue one kind of transport document. The combined transport can be categorized as Vessel Operating Common Carrier (VOCC) or Non-Vessel Operating Common Carrier

(NVOCC) based on the position of the contracting person. VOCC means that the airline companies would organize the transportation, while in NVOCC, the forwarders organize the means of transport.

3 Marine Transport

3-1 Sea Fare

Sea fare includes liner fare and charter fare. First, let's study the liner fare, which consists of four types: basic fare, additional charges, surcharges, and incidental charges.

Basic fares are based on different computation methods of FCL and LCL Cargo. For FCL cargo, the box rate would be used; for LCL Cargo, Freight Ton would be applied. The box rate for FCL cargo means that one container would be charged a fixed amount. Here, the commodity box rate is computed for each container of each article. Freight All Kinds Box Rate, which is more popular, calculates for each container and does not take each article into consideration.

Figure 12 Composition of Liner ship fare

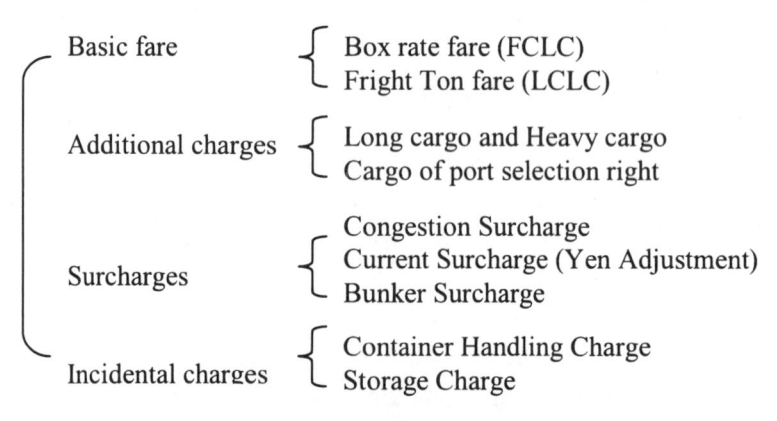

```
              ┌ Basic fare          ┤ Box rate fare (FCLC)
              │                       Fright Ton fare (LCLC)
              │
              │ Additional charges  ┤ Long cargo and Heavy cargo
              │                       Cargo of port selection right
              │
              │                       Congestion Surcharge
              │ Surcharges          ┤ Current Surcharge (Yen Adjustment)
              │                       Bunker Surcharge
              │
              │ Incidental charges  ┤ Container Handling Charge
              └                       Storage Charge
```

For LCL cargo, both shipping companies and forwarders would compute per freight ton, calculated by weight ton (1,000 kg) or capacity ton ($1m^3$). One cargo would be measured in weight and capacity, and either of them is applied. That is at the shipping company's option.

Additional charges, made for the cargos' characteristics and special section transport, are added to the basic fare. The charges are adjusted and added when the cargo is heavier or longer than the standard measurements and when the freight is not displaced in a fixed place but in two or more landing places.

Surcharges are necessary charges made for various reasons that suddenly raise the fares. Additional charges are collected from a specific shipper while surcharges are collected from all of them. For instance, there are congestion surcharges for congested ports, currency surcharge for added loss in currency exchange, and bunker surcharge for suddenly raised fuel. In Japan, the Yen once abruptly rose so much that the shipping company could have Yen adjustment surcharge (YAS) for the loss in decrease of the value of the Yen. However, recently this kind of surcharge is constantly charged and thus becomes a part of the sea fare.

Moreover, incidental charges like service charges and defrayal can be claimed. Here we can have container handing charge, terminal handling charge, storage charge, and so on.

3-2 Liner Contract
In the case of the liner, the shipper would examine the Shipping Schedule and reserve shipping space for the shipping company and its agent. Specifically, the shipper would fill in the name of the product, the name of the ship, the weight, and so on in the application for space and booking note. Other conditions are fixed, so the details do not need to be discussed here.

Regardless of the tonnage booking, when the loading cannot be done for some reasons, the dead freight would be claimed from the shipping company. Therefore, the booking will be cancelled immediately when the loading is not fulfilled.

3-3   Charter Contract

In Japan, charter is used mostly for importing raw materials. There are several types of charter but the most common one is the trip charter which is used as a charter for shippers. The trip charter is a way for the ship-owner and the shipper to make a contract for either a unit of a single trip or a trip of several times. The charter contract would include more detailed conditions than the liner contract.

The charter contract is applied for through a chartering broker or directly by the shipping company or its agent. Once the contract is concluded, a fixture note which has contracted conditions would be exchanged. Afterwards, a formal charter party would be executed. It is essential to study about the terms of fares, the inboard loading fee, loading, the demurrage charge, and the early arrival fee.

In terms of fare terms, fare calculation standard, time, place, and method of payment are agreed upon. Fare standards can be determined either by the number of loading ton, units of trips or units of days. The time of payment could be pre or post-payment; the payment place could be the loading place, handling place or others. Payment methods could be in cash or in others ways. The currency to be used must also be determined.

The inboard loading fee would determine whether the ship-owner or shipper would be responsible for the expenses related to freight loading and unloading. Here, there are fixed conditions. First, Liner Terms and Berth Terms mean that the ship-owners would be in charge of loading and unloading. This is the norm in the liner but is not used much in charter. Next, Free In and Out (FIO) mean that the ship-owners would not bear the expenses of loading and unloading. "Free" means that the ship-owner can avoid the responsibility; "in" means loading and "out" unloading. "Free In" means the shippers would avoid loading and unloading on the ship-owners. "Free Out" means the opposite; loading on ship-owners and unloading on shippers.

Loading terms include the period of anchorage at ports and

computation methods of that period. The two major methods are limited and unlimited methods. Customary Quick Dispatch (CQD) follows the port custom and does not specify the number of days. Running Laydays is the successive calculation method for the anchorage period from the first to the last day, regardless of rainy days and holidays. Weather Working Days calculates only the days that make loading possible. In the contract, 5 Running Laydays and 5 WWD would be settled.

Thus in the charter contract, the anchorage period for loading and unloading would be decided beforehand. If actual loading takes longer than scheduled, the shipper would pay the demurrage as a penalty to the ship-owner. Also, in the case where the loading finishes ahead of schedule, the ship-owner would pay the dispatch money to the shipper as a bounty. The amount of payment for demurrage or early arrival would be determined in the contract.

3-4 Bill of Lading and Sea Waybill
3-4-1 Characters of Bill of Lading

In maritime transport, there are many cases where the shipping companies would issue a Bill of Lading to the shipper after the cargo is loaded. The Bill of Lading is the document of title promising to hand over the freight to the owner, the receipt proving that the shipping company has obtained the freight, as evidence of the transport contract concluded by the shipper and the shipping company.

The Bill of Lading is the document of title, which would transfer the ownership of the freight based on the handing over of the document. In fact, the owner of the Bill of Lading is the owner of the freight. In trade payment, many times the banks are asked to attach the Bill of Lading and insurance documents to the commercial invoice, and to purchase and collect the Bill of Exchange as a documentary bill. The importer would get the Bill of Lading once he pays for it or

Format 7: Bill of Lading

Shipper KURUME SHINKO CO. INC 3-4-5 HIGASHI-MACHI, KURUME FUKUOKA, 830-0011, JAPAN	**B/L No.** NGHCC001 1E

萬海航運股份有限公司
WAN HAI LINES LTD.
BILL OF LADING

Consignee
TO ORDER OF SHIPPER

Notify party carrier not to be responsible for failure to notify
PROTRADE, THE UNION OF MANUFACTORIES
PRODUCING AND TRADING GOODS
THUAN AN DISTRICT BINH DUONG PROVINCE
TEL: 084-65-855914

Pre-carriage by	Place of receipt NAGOYA CY
Ocean vessel Voy No. WAN HAI 165 S037	Port of loading NAGOYA, JAPAN
Port of discharge HOCHIMINH CITY, VIETNAM	Place of delivery HOCHIMINH CITY CY

Container No. Seal No. Marks and Numbers	Number of containers or packages	Kind of Packages; Description of goods	Gross weight Kgs./lbs.	Measurement M³/cft.
N/M WHLU 9405320 WH 00 726364	1 CONTAINER (10 PALLETS)	"SHIPPER'S LOAD & COUNT" "SAID TO CONTAIN" SHINKO BOND E-20210 20 KGS X 600 CARTONS	12,820	24.188

Total No. of container or packages (in words)
ONE (1) CONTAINER ONLY "FREIGHT PREPAID" "AS ARRANGED"

ORIGINAL

Freight	Weight Measurement	Rate	Per	Prepaid	Collect
E.CHC	20'X1		BOX	¥11,000	

CHARGES

Carrier's Reference			3221-31		TOTAL	
Service RCV DEL'Y	Type of Goods		Freight prepaid at NAGOYA, JAPAN	Freight payable at	Place and date of issue NAGOYA, JAPAN	FEB -9 2001
1 CY 1 CY	1 ORD		Ex. Rate	No. of original B(s)/L THREE (3)	WAN HAI LINES (JAPAN), LTD.	
2 CFS 2 CFS	2 REEF				CENTRAL SHIPPING AGENCY, LTD	
3 DOOR 3 DOOR	3 DANG					

WH B/L	Date	Laden on board FEB -9 2001	Signature	By AS AGENTS

AS AGENTS FOR THE CARRIER – WAN HAI LINES LTD

promises to pay in the future. Moreover, the bank of the importer can use the Bill of Lading as a mortgage for loan and as credit to the importers. The Bill of Lading is often used for buying and selling in speculative dealings involving crude oil, sugar, grain, and rare metal.

The Bill of Lading is the receipt of the freight showing that there was no breakdown at the export or import ports and no problem when loading the cargo onboard. The receiver can then collect the freight as described in the Bill of Lading. If the quantity is deficient and the cargo is damaged, in principle, the shipping company must take the responsibility.

The Bill of Lading is the evidence of transport contract but is not the contract itself. The contract is already made before the Bill of Lading; even if there is no Bill of Lading, it can be valid as an agreement at the time of contract.

The description and interpretation of the Bill of Lading was regulated by international agreements Hague Rules made in 1921 and revised into Hague Visby Rules in 1968.

3-4-2 Types of Bill of Lading

The Bill of Lading can be divided into several types. Here we will explore the Order B/L and Straight B/L, Shipped B/L and Received B/L, Clean B/L and Foul B/L, Through B/L, Charter Party B/L and Forwarder B/L.

The Order B/L does not state the name of the specific receiver as the consignee of the B/L, but instead writes "To Order" or "To Order to Shipper". In this B/L, the names of the transferor and transferee could be written as Special Endorsement in the B/L; if there is only the name of the transferor, it would be a Blank Endorsement.

On the other hand, Straight B/L states the name of a specific consignee such as the importer. In Anglo-Saxon Law, Straight B/L is not a document of title. If the person can prove himself as the consignee written in the B/L, he can take delivery of the cargo.

The Shipped B/L is issued to confirm that the cargo is actually loaded onboard. In the ship where the shipper is responsible until the cargo is loaded, this B/L would be based on the Mate's Receipt confirming the cargo loaded.

On the other hand, Received B/L does not confirm the loading onboard, but is based on the delivery of the cargo to the carrier. The B/L of the containerized cargo is issued based on the dock receipt proving that the carrier has received the cargo at the container yard and the container freight station. Therefore, the container B/L is a Received B/L. However, in business, the person who confirms the actual container loading date and signs on the B/L would issue it in the form of Shipped B/L. This method is called on board notation.

Let us explore the difference between Clean and Foul B/L. When no problems with the quality, quantity, packing, and container externals of the cargo are found when loading it on the ship, the B/L would be a Clean B/L. In a Clean B/L, there will be no writing breakdown recapitulation on the dock receipt and the original B/L. Nevertheless, in case a problem is found in the cargo and the container, the B/L would be issued with the remarks of the problem; this is called Foul B/L. In the letter of credit, the bank would reject the Foul B/L and will not accept the payment guarantee. Therefore, the shipper would submit the Letter of Indemnity to the shipping company, meaning that he would bear the responsibility of the problems concerning the cargo. Then he can receive a Clean B/L.

If only one set of B/Ls is able to cover the whole transportation process from the export place to the import destination, it is called Through B/L. In the form of through transport, various means of transportation would be combined. The document issued for combined transport is Combined Transport Documents.

The Charter Party B/L is the B/L issued on the charter with the detailed stipulation omitted. This is called Short Form B/L as well.

The forwarder would ship the consolidated cargo instead of the shipping company. The forwarder would combine the small size cargo required by the shipper into one large size freight and ask the shipping company to ship it. This forwarder would issue the Forwarder's B/L.

3-4-3 Bill of Lading Crisis and Sea Waybill

The B/L is included in the bill of exchange sent from the exporter's bank to the importer's bank. The importer can get the B/L by paying its bank directly or promising to pay, and thus can receive the goods with the B/L. However, due to the speeding up of the ships, the goods may arrive at the import ports before the B/L reaches the importer's bank. As B/L is the document of title, the cargo cannot be received from the shipping company without the B/L. This is called B/L Crisis.

When the B/L arrives late, the cargo can be collected with a double guarantee from the bank or a single guarantee without the bank's assurance submitted to shipping company. Yet, in the case of double guarantee, the importer has to pay the guarantee fees according to the guarantee period. There are cases when the person who possesses the original B/L appears and asks for the cargo after the shipping company delivers the cargo to the person guaranteed. This cargo guarantee has such problems and there are cases where the shipping company may refuse to deliver.

Instead of the B/L, a sea waybill is used as a way to solve the B/L crisis. The sea waybill is evidential documents as a receipt of the cargo, but is not document of title. Thus it is not necessary to present the bill to collect the cargo; instead he just needs to prove himself as the person named in the sea waybill. In practice, the arrival notice is used for evidence. Another way is the Surrendered B/L. The shipping company collects this Bill without handing the B/L from the export country to the import country. Consequently, it can act as the document of title, like the sea waybill.

Although the sea waybill and Surrendered B/L can solve the B/L crisis, their disadvantages are that the cargo cannot be resold with these B/Ls. Furthermore, from the bank's viewpoint; they cannot be used as collateral documents.

Format 8: Sea Waybill

Shipper: KURUME SHINKO CO. INC 3-4-5 HIGASHI-MACHI, KURUME FUKUOKA, 830-0011, JAPAN	**Waybill No.** **NYK LINE** NIPPON YUSEN KAISHA **WAYBILL** **NON-NEGOTIABLE**
Consignee: THE COMMERCIAL BANK OF VIETNAM HOCHIMINH P5H4 DAI HOC SU PHAM 1, QUAN HOA CAU GIAY, HOCHIMINH, VIETNAM	
Notify Party: PROTRADE P8G3 THUAN AN DISTRCT BINH DUONG PROVINCE VIETNAM	RECEIVED by the Carrier from the Shipper named herein in apparent good order and condition unless otherwise indicated herein, the Goods, or the container(s) or package(s) said to contain the Goods herein mentioned, to be carried subject to the terms and conditions on the back hereof by the vessel named herein or any substitute at the Carrier's option and/or other means of transport, from the place of receipt or the port of loading to the port of discharge or the place of delivery shown herein and there to be delivered unto the Consignee named herein, or his authorized agents, on production of such proof of identity as required by the Carrier. In witness whereof, the undersigned, on behalf of Nippon Yusen Kaisha as carriers, has signed the number of Waybill(s) stated under, all of this tenor and date.
Pre-carriage by	**Place of Receipt**: NAGOYA CY
Ocean Vessel: SAKURA MARU **Voy. No.**: N668	**Port of Loading**: NAGOYA JAPAN
Port of Discharge: HOCHIMINH VIETNAM	**Place of Delivery**: HOCHIMINH CY	**Final destination (for the Merchant's reference only)**

Container No.	Seal No. Marks & Nos.	No. of Containers or P'kgs.	Kind of Packages; Description of Goods	Gross Weight	Measurement
N/M WHLU 9402381	WH 00 76579	1 CONTAINER	"SHIPPER'S LOAD & COUNT" "SAID TO CONTAIN" SHINKO BOND E-20210 20KGS X 600 CARTONS "FREIGHT PREPAID" "AS ARRANGED"	12,820	24,188

(*)TOTAL NUMBER OF CONTAINERS,
PACKAGES OR UNITS(IN WORDS)

FREIGHT & CHARGES	Revenue Tons	Rate	Per	Prepaid	Collect
E.CHC		20' X 1	BOX	23,000	

	Ex. Rate	Prepaid at: NAGOYA, JAPAN	Payable at	Place of Waybill(s) Issue: NAGOYA, JAPAN	Dated: FEB 7, 2001
ICS B/L		Total Prepaid in Local Currency	Number of Original Waybills: THREE (3)	**NIPPON YUSEN KAISHA**	

Laden on Board the Vessel
Date: FEB 9, 2001   By

Form No. C-1018F   (JSA STANDARD FORM A)   (TERMS CONTINUED ON BACK HEREOF)

B/L and other shipment documents in form of electronic data are applicable as well. This method can solve the B/L crisis since the shipping documents can be sent from the exporter's banks to the importer's banks immediately. Still, more time is needed for this to be used commonly.

4   Air Transport

4-1   Air Fare

Air cargo is composed of direct cargo and consolidated cargo. Direct cargo is to be shipped directly by the airline company; the cargo would be contracted with its air cargo agent. The consolidated cargo involves the consolidator, not the airline company directly. That consolidator would combine cargoes of different shippers into a consolidated large sized cargo as a contract carrier and ask the airline company for carriage. In main air routes, almost all of the cargo is consolidated cargo.

The fare of direct cargo to each area is set by the International Air Transport Association (IATA) and is called IATA Fare. The fare decided independently by a non-member airline company is called non-IATA Fare. Let's study the system of the IATA Fare. There is much difference between the fixed fare and the actual fare. Users of direct fare are mostly consolidators.

IATA Fare includes the lowest fee, general cargo fare rate, fee per pallet or container, specific commodity rate, commodity classification rate, and value charges. General cargo fare rate is not related to the commodity, but the cargo that cannot be stuffed into the container. Each unit is on freight-kg, which means it can be computed by the kg of weight or m^3 of capacity.

The fee per pallet or container is calculated by the pallet and or container loaded with the cargo.

Format 9: Air Waybill

Shipper's Name and Address	Shipper's Account Number	Not negotiable **Air Waybill**
KURUME SHINKO CO. INC 3-4-5 HIGASHI-MACHI, KURUME FUKUOKA, 830-0011, JAPAN		Issued by **EXPRESS FORWARDING INC.**

Consignee's Name and Address	Consignee's Account Number	Copies 1, 2 and 3 of this Air Waybill are originals and have the same validity.
THE COMMERCIAL BANK OF VIETNAM HOCHIMINH P5H4 DAI HOC SU PHAM 1, QUAN HOA CAU GIAY, HOCHIMINH, VIETNAM		It is agreed that the goods described herein are accepted in apparent good order and condition (except as noted) for carriage SUBJECT TO THE CONDITIONS OF CONTRACT ON THE REVERSE HEREOF. ALL GOODS MAY BE CARRIED BY ANY OTHER MEANS INCLUDING ROAD OR ANY OTHER CARRIER UNLESS SPECIFIC CONTRARY INSTRUCTIONS ARE GIVEN HEREON BY THE SHIPPER, AND SHIPPER AGREES THAT THE SHIPMENT MAY BE CARRIED VIA INTERMEDIATE STOPPING PLACES WHICH THE CARRIER DEEMS APPROPRIATE. THE SHIPPER'S ATTENTION IS DRAWN TO THE NOTICE CONCERNING CARRIER'S LIMITATION OF LIABILITY. Shipper may increase such limitation of liability by declaring a higher value for carriage and paying a supplemental charge if required.

Issuing Carrier's Name and City	Accounting Information
EXPRESS FORWARDING INC., FUKUOKA	

Airport of Departure (Addr. of First Carrier) and Requested Routing: **FUK-HAN**

To	By First Carrier	Routing and Destination	to	by	to	by	Currency	Chgs Code	WT VAL	Other	Declared Value for Carriage	Declared Value for Customs
HAN	JAL						USD		CC PP	CC PP	NVD	

Airport of Destination	Requested Flight/Date	Amount of Insurance	If shipper requests insurance in accordance with the conditions thereof, indicate amount to be insured in figures in box marked "Amount of Insurance"
HANOI	JAL786/2.7		

Handling Information

No. of Pieces RCP	Gross Weight	kg/lb	Rate Class / Commodity Item No.	Chargeable Weight	Rate / Charge	Total	Nature and Quantity of Goods (incl. Dimensions or Volume)
8	200.6	K	C 6750	201	1.90	381.90	SHINKO BOND
8	200.6						

Prepaid	Weight Charge	Collect	Other Charges
	381.90		
	Valuation Charge		
	Tax		
	Total other Charges Due Agent		Shipper certifies that the particulars on the face hereof are correct and agrees THE CONDITIONS ON THE REVERSE HEREOF.
	15.00		
	Total other Charges Due Carrier		EXPRESS FORWARDING INC.
			Signature of Shipper or his Agent
Total Prepaid		Total Collect	Carrier certifies that the goods described hereon are accepted for carriage subject to THE CONDITION OF CONTRACT ON THE REVERSE HEREOF, the goods then being in apparently good order and condition except as noted hereon.
396.90			
Currency Conversion Rates		CC Charges in Dest. Currency	FEB 7 FUKUOKA EXPRESS FORWARDING INC
			Executed on (date) at (place) Signature of Issuing Carrier
For Carriers Use only at Destination		Charges at Destination	
		Total Collect Charges	

COPY   PRINTED IN JAPAN

Specific commodity rates are for particular commodities from a specified point of origin to a specified destination point while the classification rate is surcharged or reduced rate for particular commodities. Value charges are for high value commodities. However, when the transport contract does not declare the amount of value, the value charge cannot be collected. This is called "No Value Declared"(N.V.D.).

Though consolidate cargo fare is determined independently by consolidators, in general, there are general cargo rates rate and specific commodity rates. Compared with Direct Cargo Fare, as Consolidate Cargo Fare has a cheaper rate for low-weight, consolidating is more advantageous for small sized freight.

4-2 Air Transport Contract and Air Waybill

As mentioned above, the air cargo agent, not the airline company, makes the air cargo transport contract. To IATA member airline companies, their agents are also authorized by the IATA and are called IATA air cargo agent.

The shipper and the air cargo agent would make a contract on the direct cargo. When the agent receives the freight, he would issue air waybill; strictly speaking, the shipper is supposed to delivery it.

The shipper and the consolidator would contract the consolidated cargo. The consolidator would combine small size freight for each destination into one large size and ask the air cargo agent for carriage. The agent would issue the air waybill of the airline company to the consolidator. To differentiate the two sides, the bill of the airline company is called the master air waybill and the bill of the consolidator, the house air waybill.

The air waybill is characterized as a receipt of the freight and is evidence of the transport contract. However, as air cargo would arrive at the destination in a short amount of time, the air waybill is not negotiable; thus it is not the document of title. This is the main difference with the bill of lading.

5 Combined Transport

5-1 Combined Transport Fare
Combined transport includes various means of transportation like ships, planes, trains, and trucks. In export from Japan, there are land bridges combining ships, trains and trucks, and a combination of sea and air for ships and planes.

The land bridge is common in fixed routes like the Siberia Land Bridge and the America Land Bridge. The fare would be fixed per container. The sea-air is not specialized for fixed routes. Anywhere is possible if there is a relay port near the airport. Thus, the fare is not fixed but combined by the sea fare and the air fare.

5-2 Combined Transport Contract and Documents
Combined transport contract shows shipping companies with the means of transport and coordinates all transportation section that consists of transporters and those who do not have means of transport. The documents issued are called combined transport documents. The Combined Transport B/L and the sea waybill are both issued. Though B/L is document of title, the sea waybill issued is not.

Combined transport possesses various means of transport. Each transporter would bear independent transport responsibility. Thus if accidents occur in shipment, how the transporter would take responsibility is important for the shipper as well.

Responsibility is not unified in combined transport. The main principle is that the shipper and those who contracted would bear the same responsibility in the whole transport section. This is called uniform liability system. Although the contractor is in charge of the whole section, the content would be based on the responsibility of each

Format 10: Combined Transport Document

					(Forwarding Agent)	
Shipper KURUME SHINKO CO. INC 3-4-5 HIGASHI-MACHI, KURUME FUKUOKA, 830-0011, JAPAN				JIFFA	B/L No.	
				MULTIMODAL TRANSPORT BILL OF LADING		
Consignee TO ORDER OF SHIPPER				SANKYU INC.		
Notify Party PROTRADE P8G3 THUAN AN DISTRCT BINH DUONG PROVINCE VIETNAM TEL:086-65-85594				Received by the Carrier from the shipper in apparent good order and condition unless otherwise indicated herein, the Goods, or the container(s) or package(s) said to contain the cargo herein mentioned, to be carried subject to all the terms and conditions appearing on the face and back of this Bill of Lading by the vessel named herein or any substitute at the Carrier's option and/or other means of transport, from the place of receipt or the port of loading to the port of discharge or the place of delivery shown herein and there to be delivered unto order or assigns. This Bill of Lading duly endorsed must be surrendered in exchange for the Goods or delivery order. In accepting this Bill of Lading, the Merchant agrees to be bound by all the stipulations, exceptions terms and conditions on the face and back hereof, whether written, typed, stamped or printed, as fully as if signed by the Merchant, any local custom or privilege to the contrary notwithstanding, and agrees that all agreements or freight engagements for and in connection with the carriage of the Goods are superseded by this Bill of Lading.		
Pre-carriage by		Place of Receipt NAGOYA CY		Party to contact for cargo release		
Vessel WAI HAI 165	Voy. No. S037	Port of Loading NAGOYA JAPAN				
Port of Discharge HOCHIMINH VIETNAM		Place of Delivery PROTRADE WAREHOUSE (THUAN AN DISTRICT)		Final Destination (Merchant's reference only)		
Container No. Seal No. Marks and Numbers		No. of Containers or Pkgs	Kind of Packages: Description of Goods		Gross Weight	Measurement
N/M WHLU 9402381 WH 00 76529		1 CONTAINER	"SHIPPER'S LOAD & COUNT" "SAID TO CONTAIN" SHINKO BOND E-20210 20KGS X 600 CARTONS "FREIGHT PREPAID" "AS ARRANGED"		12,820	24,188
Total number of Containers or other Packages or Units (in words)		1 CONTAINER				
Merchant's Declared Value (See Clauses 18 & 23): N.V.D.			Note The Merchant's attention is called to the fact that according to Clauses 18 & 23 of this Bill of Lading the liability of the Carrier is, in most cases, limited in respect of loss of or damage to the Goods.			
Freight and Charges		Revenue Tons	Rate	Per	Prepaid	Collect
E.CHC			20'X 1	BOX	23,000	
Exchange Rate	Prepaid at NAGOYA, JAPAN		Payable at		Place and Date of Issue NAGOYA, JAPAN FEB 7, 2001	
	Total Prepaid in Local Currency		No. of Original B(s)/L THREE (3)		In witness whereof, the undersigned has signed the number of Bill(s) of Lading stated herein, all of this tenor and date, one of which being accomplished, the others to stand void.	
Vessel WAI HAI 165 S037		Laden on Board the Vessel Date FEB 7, 2001			As Carrier SANKYU INC.	
Port of Loading NAGOYA, JAPAN		By *(signature)*			*(signature)*	
An enlarged copy of back clauses is available from the Carrier upon request.		(TERMS CONTINUED ON BACK HEREOF) © JIFFA MODEL FORM (19-5-2000)			DUPLICATE	

means of transport as of the network liability system; the transporters would be responsible in each section as in the divided liability system.

Questions

1 Explain the relationship between trade terms and the importer's transportation arrangement.
2 Explain the function of the forwarder.
3 Explain the characters of B/L and its functions in trade payment.
4 Explain the B/L Crisis and effective solutions.
5 The majority of air transport is consolidated cargo. Consolidated cargo is also increasing in maritime transport. Discuss in class possible problems that may occur when consolidators play both the roles of the shipping company and air cargo agent.

Chapter 3
Insurance Arrangement

Summary

In trade payment, there are insurances to avoid several risks. In this chapter, we will study cargo insurance for cargo damage in transit, trade insurance for risk of companies' incapability in case of bankruptcy or wars, and product liability (PL) insurance.

1 Cargo Insurance

1-1 Necessity of Cargo Insurance

If using the CIF terms in the sales contract, the seller would obtain the cargo insurance, and must hand over the insurance policy to the buyer. In other trade terms, the insurance contract is not required for in sales contracts. However, it is preferable that the seller or buyer prepares the insurance for himself for the following reasons.

Trade cargo is internationally transported and is exposed to various risks compared to domestic transport. Therefore, there is a high chance of the cargo being damaged. The shipping company is responsible for safe cargo shipment and the shipper is responsible for any damage that occurs in the transport process.

However, the shipping company is usually not responsible in the provisions of the B/L when the cargo damage is caused by a ship loss, a ship fire, sea risks, natural disasters, wars, riots, civil commotions, strikes, and piracy, character of cargo and hidden defects, and imperfect shipping marks. Moreover, even though the damage compensation is to be made, the amount is limited and payment tends to be delayed.

If the cargo is insured, the insurance company pays the

insurance or loan as substantial insurance money even though the responsibility of shipping company is not clear or the damage compensation payment is delayed.

For these reasons, the cargo needs to be insured in order to avoid the risks occurring in the transport process. As mentioned before, in CIF and CIP, the seller is obliged to obtain the insurance for the buyer; in other contracts, it is also necessary to insure it for themselves.

1-2 Terminologies of Cargo Insurance

There are several terms for insurances in insurance contracts. Let's study these expressions.

First, we will discuss the insurer and the insured. The insurer would pay for the insurance based on the insurance contracts. In Britain and America, individuals can be an insurer; in Japan, however, only a corporate as an insurance company can be an insurer. The insured would pay the insurance fee and has the rights to collect the insurance when the cargo is damaged. The ordinary insurer and insured can be the same, but in the CIF contract, the exporter would procure the insurance and hand the insurance policy to the importer. Thus, the importer is the insured.

In cargo insurance, the cargo is called subject-matter insured. Interest related to the insured cargo is insurable interest. This interest can be called the interest of the cargo owner. If there is no insurable interest, the damage compensation cannot be paid.

The amount of insurable interest is expressed as insurable value, computed at the current price. The insured amount is determined in the insurance contract and the highest amount that is paid by the insurer when there is damage. If the insured amount falls below the insurable value, it is called under insurance. If the insured amount equals the insured value, it is called full insurance; if the insured amount exceeds, it is called over insurance. The excess is not insurable interest and thus cannot be paid. Normally, under insurance or over insurance does not emerge as both the insured amount and the insurable value are obtained by adding 10% interests onto the cargo amount calculated by CIF. The insurer would abide the risks to the cargo transported for the Insured, and thus the fee for bearing this risk is called insurance premium, paid by the insured to the insurer. The premium is the insurance rate calculated by the insured amount. The insurance is the redemption paid by the insurer to the insured in the case of cargo damage.

1-3 Insurance Policy
The present insurance policies are the old insurance policy and the new insurance policy. The contents from any insurance companies would be the same since each insurance company in the world patterns after the standards of the Institute of London Underwriters.

The history of the old insurance policy goes back to the Lloyd's SG Form, which was made by the London Maritime Insurance Market in 1779. The old insurance policy includes three terms: Free From Particular Average (FPA), With Average (WA) and All Risks.

The old policy was criticized as being hard to understand and the Institute of London Underwriters enacted the new policy in 1982. The three instituted cargo clauses A, B, C are set for Free from Particular Average, With Average, and All Risks, respectively.

Yet, in England and several countries, and in the insurance market of the world, the old policy is still popular. The new policy is based on the old policy. Here a discussion of the old policy will be followed by the new policy.

1-4 Insurance Conditions
1-4-1 Risk and Damage
The cargo transported is exposed to various risks. It is possible that these risks will cause damage to the cargo.

Format 11: Insurance Policy

THE KOA FIRE & MARINE INSURANCE COMPANY, LIMITED
HEAD OFFICE: 7-3, 3-CHOME, KASUMIGASEKI, CHIYODA-KU, TOKYO, JAPAN. (INCORPORATED IN JAPAN)

CABLE "KOAKASAI TOKYO"
TELEX KOAINS J23524

Assured, etc.
KURUME SHINKO CO. INC
3-4-5 HIGASHI-MACHI, KURUME
FUKUOKA, 830-0011, JAPAN

Invoice No. K-010117

POLICY No. 5200-023977

Amount insured ¥1,320,000.-

Claim, if any, payable at in
HOCHIMINH CITY INSURANCE COMPANY
(BAO MINH)
by 26 TON THAT DAM STREET,
DISTRICT 1, HOCHIMINH CITY.
TEL. (8) 8294180, 8230181
FAX. (8) 8294185

Conditions:
AGAINST ALL RISKS
INCLUDING WAR & S.R.C.C.

Ship or Vessel called the
WAN HAI 165

at and from
NAGOYA, JAPAN

Sailing on or about
FEB. 9, 2001

thence to
HOCHIMINH, VIETNAM

Goods and Merchandises
600 CARTONS OF SHINKO BOND

IN CONTAINER(S) TO BE STOWED ON &/OR UNDER DECK

Including risks of War and Strikes, Riots & Civil Commotions.
Subject to the following Clauses printed on the back hereof:
Institute Cargo Clauses.
Institute War Clauses (Cargo).
Institute Strikes Riots and Civil Commotion Clauses
Institute Replacement Clause (applying to machinery)
Institute Dangerous Drugs Clause.
Duty Clause (applying only to duty insured).

Marks and Numbers as per Invoice No. specified above.
Place and Date signed in NAGOYA JAN. 24, 2001
Valued at the same as Amount insured.
No. of Policies issued TWO

Be it known, That

In witness whereof, I the Undersigned of THE KOA FIRE AND MARINE INSURANCE COMPANY, LIMITED, on behalf of the said Company, have subscribed my Name in to Policies of the same tenor and date, one of which being accomplished, the others to be void, as of the date specified as above.

For **THE KOA FIRE AND MARINE INSURANCE COMPANY, LIMITED.**

AUTHORIZED SIGNATORY K. Yokoyama

Examined

The reasons and consequences are expressed as risks and damages. Risks, based on the insurance policy, includes voyage risks (in particular, maritime risks, fire, burglar, wreckage, bad behaviors of captains and crews, abnormality and similar risks); war and strikes, riots and civil commotions risk; extraneous risks besides War & SRCC (robbery: non – delivery; dangerous contacts of manuscript: oil, mud, acid, and others; damage by bending, leakage, rain, sweat, getting stuffy, natural fires, and mold); and perils not covered in the insurance (quality and defect of original product, transport delay, imperfect packing, dangerous nuclear power).

Figure 13   Types of Risk

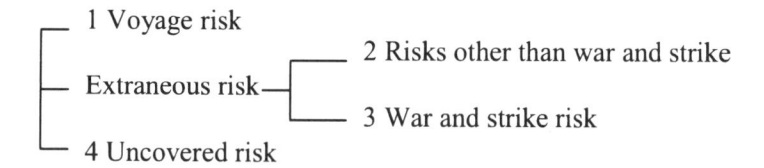

```
┌─ 1 Voyage risk
│                      ┌─ 2 Risks other than war and strike
├─ Extraneous risk ─┤
│                      └─ 3 War and strike risk
└─ 4 Uncovered risk
```

Moreover, the level of consequences is shown in Figure 14. The total loss is the loss of all the insured cargo under which actual total loss means that the cargo is completely destroyed; on the other hand, constructive total loss is when the ship is missing and the total loss is estimated or when the cargo is partial lost and the cost of repair and storage exceeds the remaining value of the cargo. In this case, the procedure is regarded as a total loss.

Partial loss is when a part of the cargo value covered by the insurance contract is damaged. General average is the damage when the ship and cargo abandons a part of cargo and saves the total value in case of risks. In general average other cargo is sacrificed so all of the shippers are evenly responsible.

Particular average is when a part of the cargo damaged. Its difference with general average is that only the shipper of the damaged cargo is responsible. Moreover, particular average is divided into specific loss (damages because of running aground, sinking and conflagration of ship and barge; of the collision between ships and with other transportation tools; and of lowering the cargo) and other unspecific loss.

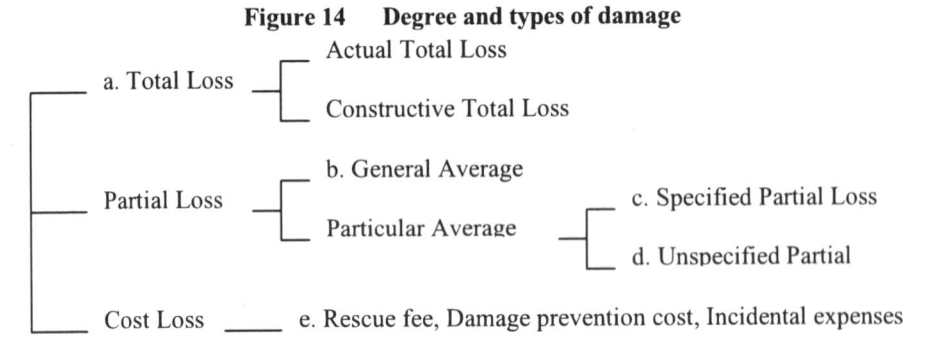

Figure 14 Degree and types of damage

```
                            ┌─ Actual Total Loss
         ┌─ a. Total Loss ──┤
         │                  └─ Constructive Total Loss
         │
         │                     ┌─ b. General Average
 ────────┤   Partial Loss ─────┤                            ┌─ c. Specified Partial Loss
         │                     └─ Particular Average ───────┤
         │                                                  └─ d. Unspecified Partial
         │
         └─ Cost Loss ──── e. Rescue fee, Damage prevention cost, Incidental expenses
```

In addition, there are rescue fees to scoop the ship and the cargo, damage prevention costs to prevent the damage from expanding, and incidental expenses to investigate the damage.

The contents insurance conditions are determined based on the types of risks, level and types of damages discussed above.

1-4-2 Contents of Insurance Conditions

There are three types of insurance conditions: Free From Particular Average (FPA), With Average (WA), and All Risks. The same insurance condition is applied because international insurance companies apply the same insurance policy.

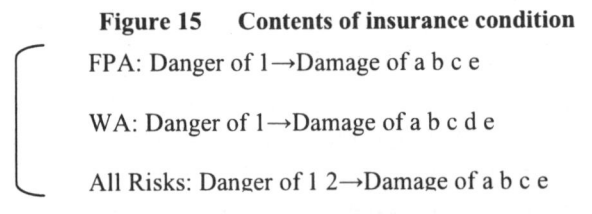

Figure 15 Contents of insurance condition

```
    ┌─ FPA: Danger of 1→Damage of a b c e
    │
    ├─ WA: Danger of 1→Damage of a b c d e
    │
    └─ All Risks: Danger of 1 2→Damage of a b c e
```

Free from particular average, as shown in Figure 15, is provision for the damage in the case of partial loss, general average, and specific loss due to maritime risks. As understood in English terms, this provision does not compensate for particular average, but only for specific loss.

With average is provision for the damage in the case of total loss, general average and particular average due to maritime risks. It will pay off the unspecific partial loss that cannot be compensated by FPA. However, the range of unspecified partial loss would be narrowed down and limited to damage done by the tide. Thus, FPA and WA are different by the compensation of the damage of the tide.

WA is limited to the amount that exceeds the fixed rate for the redeemed damage. This is called franchise. But in general, regardless of franchise, if "Irrespective of percentage" is added to the insurance policy, it can also be compensated within the range of the franchise.

All risks is provision compensation for damages caused by maritime risks, in addition to accompanied risks like wars, strikes, total loss, general average and particular average. Though wars and strikes are covered by extraneous risks, they are special contracted risks so it is necessary to apply separately.

1-5 Insurance Period

Insurance period is the length of time the insurer can compensate for the damage. It is mentioned in Article 1 on the back of the old policy and Article 8 in the Transit Clause of the new policy.

According to the Transit Clause, the insurance period is from departure at the exporter's warehouse to arrival at the importer's warehouse. There is a limit of 60 days from the time when the cargo is loaded at the import port. Also, when it is delivered at the storage place and warehouse that are not the final stop, the insurance period would end even if it is not the final warehouse.

The insurance period follows the warehouse-to-warehouse principle. The insurance period can be shortened based on the trade terms in the sales contract. For instance, in FOB, when the cargo is loaded on the ship of export port moor, the seller completes the delivery to the buyer, and then the risks are transferred. Therefore, since the importer is not insured from the seller's warehouse to the ship in export port, the risks are not covered by the insurance contracted by the buyer. In FOB contract, the insurance period for the buyer is from the ship at the export port to the seller's final warehouse.

In FOB and C&F, when importer procures the cargo insurance, the insurance company would stamp the insurance policy "FOB Attachment Clause" as a specific provision for attention.

When using FOB and C&F, the insurance by the importer cannot cover the risks from the exporter's first warehouse to the ship at the export port. For the exporter, the export FOB insurance is available as a domestic insurance.

1-6 Conditions of New Insurance Policy

The new insurance policy includes Institute Cargo Clause (ICC) A, B and C. ICC (A) is constituted from the standards of All Risks of the old policy. In All Risks, the insurance does not pay for the damage based on peculiar malfeasance and deliberate defects and characteristics in the freight of the Insured; these are called excluded perils. In ICC (A), the damage caused from insufficient packing and insolvency of the ship owners becomes an exemption as well.

ICC (B) is for WA. However, in the new policy, the danger provision itself runs out. As a result, maritime risk would also disappear. On the other hand, the danger instead would cover the risks of seawater invasion in means of transport like ships and containers. In addition to the immunity reasons of ICC (A), ICC (B) excludes the damages by nuclear fission, nuclear core and harmful actions. The franchise used by partial loss of the old policy is deleted in the new policy so minor damages would be compensated for.

ICC (C) is a provision standard for FPA but since there is no specific loss, all of particular average is not compensated for.

Moreover, the insurance period in the new Policy is the same to the old one.

1-7 Cargo Insurance Contract

Insurance form is based on the Application for Marine Insurance. The insurance contractor, as a rule, is the insured; but a person who is committed by the insured may contract. As the insured has obligations to notify the conditions to be agreed on, the information in the application form must be written precisely. The insurer is the insurance company but the insurance agent usually makes the contracts. In America, there is an insurance broker between the insurer and the insured, who carries out the insurance contract. This does not exist in Japan.

The insured would fill in the necessary information in the insurance application form, and the insurer would calculate the insurance rate and present it to the insured. The insurance rate can be computed as a percentage or 100 yen per how much. The three calculation methods are Free Rate, Conventional Rate and War and Strike Rate.

In the Free Rate items, each insurance company determines competitively for the insured. Most of the export cargo and the import cargo not included in the Conventional Rate belong to this category. The Free Rate is calculated by standards of ship classification; transport section; types, characteristics, quantity of freight; damage rate for similar freight; and track record of the Insured.

The Conventional Rate is determined to prevent the excessive competition among insurance companies. All insurance companies would apply the same rate. A main part of the Conventional Rate is Major Import Cargo Tariff Agreement (MICA).

The War and Strike rate cannot be acknowledged based on the information collected at each insurance company; instead, it is calculated every week at the London War Risks Rating Committee.

The insurance companies in the world would use this rate and therefore, war and strikes risks are always specially contracted.

1-8　Insurance Documents

When the insurance contract is concluded, the insurance company would issue the insurance policy or the insurance certificate to the insured. An insurance certificate omits the details written in the insurance policy.

　　The insurance contract has to be concluded before the insurance period starts. However, when the insurance period begins, necessary conditions in the contract may not be determined yet. For example, when the importer procures the insurance, the name of vessel and the date of loading are sometimes unknown.

　　In this case, the provisional policy can be applied. Once the scheduled insurance is decided, the provisional policy or cover note can be issued. In the cover note, the detailed conditions of the scheduled insurance policy are omitted; it is the insurance certificate issued instead of the insurance policy.

　　If any thing was clarified when the scheduled insurance is concluded, it must be clearly declared to the insurer. This is called the definite declaration. Hence, the insurer would issue the insurance policy or the insurance certificate to the insured.

　　The insurance contract is done for each cargo or for each time of transport; however, in the case of long-term trading, the open policy is applied. The open policy is an insurance contract that covers the transport of freight that may be turned over in the future. Even in the open policy, if there is no definite declaration, the formal insurance policy has to be handed in.

1-9　Air Cargo Insurance

There are two methods of air cargo insurance. One is using the Institute Air Cargo Clause of marine insurance policy; the other one is to apply for shipper's interest by filling the insurance amount in the insurance column of airway bill.

Institute Air Cargo Clauses are concluded in new and old policies. The old and new policies correspond to All Risks provision. The insurance period is also from warehouse-to-warehouse. However, the insurance period is limited to 30 days after unloading.

The shipper's interest is a system used by shippers as an open insurance contract of the insurance company and the airline company. The shipper only writes the insurance amount in the insurance column of air waybill; thus the insurance would be automatically procured. This insurance is only on All Risks as well. The insurance period is from the time the airline company or its agent keeps the cargo to the time it is delivered to the consignee at the decided destination. As this insurance has a damage compensation limit, it is generally used for cargo of little sum.

2 Trade Insurance

2-1 Function of Trade Insurance

We have studied the damage insurance for cargo in the transport process. However, the trade insurance is an insurance system for the risk of contracts such as not being able to make a deal or when the payment cannot be made after the sales contract is made.

In trade transaction, the contract cannot be implemented after the sales contract is made due to risks in which the trade persons cannot bear responsibility like wars, civil commotions, strikes, import restrictions and prohibitions, and natural disasters in the import country. This danger is called emergency risks. Moreover, the contract implementation is usually impossible when the trade partners cannot pay or become bankrupt. This is called credit risk.

When there is damage caused by these risks, the government or governmental organization is the insurer because the damage amount is often large. In Japan, the Nippon Export and Investment Insurance (NEXI) and other private companies are the insurer.

2-2 Types of Trade Insurance

In Japan, as of April 2006, there are seven types of insurance according to the NEXI: general trade insurance, short-term limit amount set trade insurance (for manufacturers), export bill insurance, export policy insurance, advance payment import insurance, overseas investment insurance and overseas business fund lending insurance. Each system would be altered or terminated by societal and economical changes; the latest information can be searched for on the Nippon Trade Insurance website.

The general trade insurance is compensation for loss of exporters and intermediary traders. After the contract is concluded, the loss of exporters and intermediary traders, when loading is impossible, would be redeemed due to emergency risk or credit risk of importer. Even after the cargo is loaded, in emergency risk, when the shipping fee and the insurance fee increase due to changes in the shipping route, the increase would also be reimbursed. Besides, in the case of emergency risks and credit risks, the loss by irrevocable deposit would also be compensated.

Short-term limit amount set trade insurance (for manufacturers), for Japanese manufacturers and specific overseas traders, exporters or intermediary traders, is a compensation for the loss of loading and deposit repayment which cannot be paid for due to emergency risks and credit risks. The insurance period is one year for the object in regular dealings with a specific overseas trader. The object in sales dealings is within one year from the contract to payment; in addition, the term of the bill must be within six months. The compensation amount is limited by the insured amount in the insurance contract. As mentioned, since the insurance period is within one year, the contract fulfilled in this period would be insured. In fact, even if the actual damage occurs after the insurance period, it is acceptable that the contract is concluded within the insurance period.

The export bill insurance is an insurance system that compensates the loss of the bill negotiating banks. The banks in export country would buy the bill of the exporters. However, due to emergency risks and credit risks, the importers cannot pay the deposits; thus the bill would be dishonored. The loss of the bank would be redeemed in this insurance system. This system does not use letter of credit, but D/P and D/A payment instead.

The export policy insurance is an insurance system for the bond issued by the banks. The exporters have to submit the bond of banks for the export of plant facilities and technical cooperation. Here, the compensation is demanded based on the bond.

Advance payment import insurance is an insurance system for importers. In case the importer makes a pre-payment, due to emergency risks and credit risks, the freight cannot be imported and the loss of the pre-paid deposit would be reimbursed.

Overseas investment insurance is a compensation system for the loss due to emergency risks and credit risks to Japanese companies doing overseas investments.

Overseas business fund lending insurance is a compensation system for the loss due to emergency risks and credit risks to Japanese companies lending to overseas companies that cannot repay the loan.

3 Product Liability Insurance

3-1 What Is Product Liability

Product Liability means the manufacturers and distributors have to be liable when the consumer gets injured due to the defect product.

In the past, this responsibility was judged by the fault-based responsibility principle. In Europe and America, it is considered necessary to consider defect liability as a high possibility because of mass-production. This is called product liability.

While the fault-based liability has to prove the fault in the production phase of the manufacturers, the defect liability has to show the defect in the product itself. This is the special difference between the liability principle in the past and product liability.

In America, product liability is determined by the states; thus, the liability range may vary a little. The federal government establishes the product liability model to correct the difference, and each state would adopt that model. In the EU, the common legislation is processed based on the EU instructions. In Japan, the Product Liability Act was enforced in 1995.

3-2 Details of Product Liability Insurance

In the case where the Japanese manufacturers and exporters do not find the defect product and the exporters who make the manuals and disclaimers neglect their obligations, they must bear the compensation liability in the import country. The importers can also claim the exporters as not performing their responsibilities in the contract based on the damage compensation to the importers in the import country.

Moreover, the importers are not manufacturers, but as suppliers of the product in the country, they have to be liable along with the manufacturers and processors.

Both exporters and importers could have to bear responsibility for product liability. First, it is necessary that the manufacturers check the product quality thoroughly. The exporters have to investigate that the products comply with the display standards and safety standards of the import country. The importers would need to examine whether the products are appropriate with Japanese safety standards, and renew the manuals and disclaimers to the Japanese standards.

Yet, it is necessary to consider joining the product liability insurance as the damage compensation of product liability is sometimes large. Normally, product liability insurance is composed of domestic liability and an international one.

For example, while the Japan Chamber of Commerce and Industry offers "small and medium company PL insurance" and "small and medium companies overseas PL insurance", there is not a big difference in conditions; however, the insurance rate is different.

Since product liability insurance is compensation for damage and accidents that occur in a particular period, the limit of insured amount considering the number of accidents have to be made. The damage compensation amount is the insurance paid. Besides, such lawsuits fee and emergency treatment fee would be paid under a different limit amount.

Questions

1 Explain the necessity of cargo insurance, trade insurance, and product liability insurance.
2 Explain the important point of the cargo insurance period.
3 Discuss in class the reasons why the new insurance policy is not popular in Japan.

Chapter 4
Payment and Trade Finance Arrangement

Summary

This chapter discusses bank-related preparation. If the buyer and the seller agree to use L/C in their trade contract, the exporter should apply for issuance of the L/C to the transaction bank. Then, after the exporter receives the L/C, they must carefully examine the details of the content. In the case of payment by L/C and documentary draft, the exporter should prepare the documentary draft. Thus, in this chapter, we will study the compilation of documentary draft, some other trade finances, and avoiding foreign exchange risks. Shipping documents are discussed in each related chapter and please refer to it.

1 Letter of Credit (L/C)

1-1 What is L/C

In trade transaction, there is no guarantee that the exporter receives payment from the importer securely as long as the transaction is not made in advance. In any chance, if the importer fails to pay, there are very few payment methods for revoking the deposit; moreover, it will be difficult to revoke through legal procedures.

To avoid this kind of problem, there is a system in which the exporter's bank guarantees the importer's payment to the exporter. This system is called Letter of credit (L/C).

The L/C is not only used to avoid payment failure, but the exporter uses the L/C to require the exporter's bank to pay the exporter first on behalf of the importer. Therefore, the exporter can receive the

112 Part 2 Contract Fulfillment Preparation

payment right after the shipment. Moreover, because the L/C is issued based on the conditions stated in the contract, the importer fulfillment on L/C conditions is the fulfillment of the contract conditions.

Although the L/C has many advantages, the L/C also becomes the source for more costs for the importer. Therefore, the L/C is often used in transaction between the two independent enterprises; however, it is used less in transactions between the headquarters and branch offices or in transactions between related enterprises, in which there is no concerns about the importer's credibility.

1-2 Issuance of L/C

After the L/C payment is agreed upon in the trade contract and after the trade contract is completed, the importer should apply for issuance of the L/C to the transaction bank. However, before the issuance of the L/C, the importer needs to submit a basic agreement of commercial L/C. Moreover, for each transaction, they need to submit an application for irrevocable letter of credit.

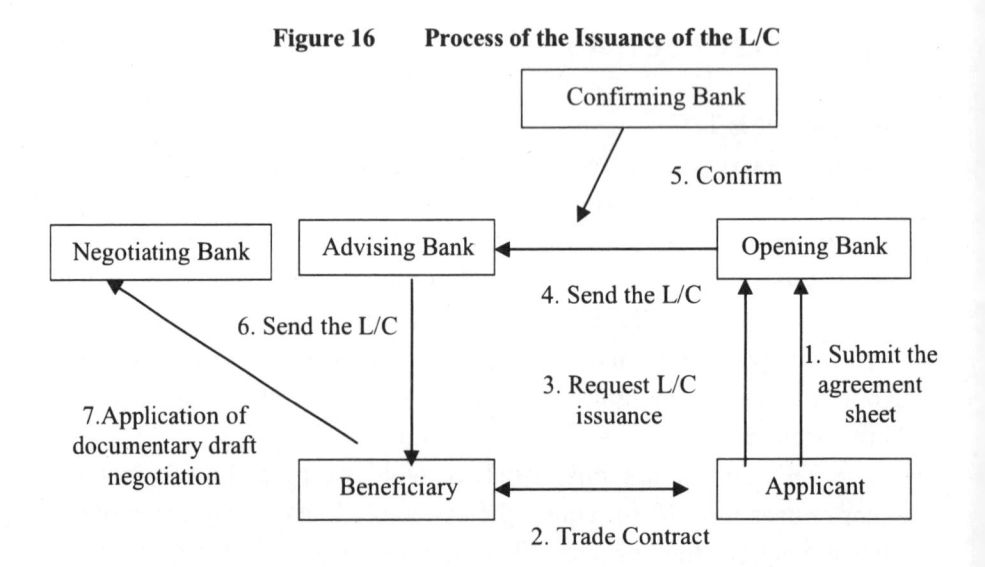

Figure 16   Process of the Issuance of the L/C

```
                         Confirming Bank
                              │
                              │  5. Confirm
                              ▼
Negotiating Bank   Advising Bank  ◄────  Opening Bank
                                  4. Send the L/C
       ▲                                   ▲   ▲
       │   6. Send the L/C                 │   │ 1. Submit the
       │                       3. Request L/C  │   agreement
   7. Application of              issuance     │   sheet
   documentary draft
       negotiation        Beneficiary  ◄────  Applicant
                                  2. Trade Contract
```

In trade transaction using the L/C, the applicant is the importer, who should apply for the issuance of the L/C to the transaction bank after the completion of the contract.

The bank that issues the L/C is called the opening bank or the issuing bank. The L/C is an important credit decision for the bank; therefore, the bank has to consider the credibility of the importer, and decide whether they will issue the L/C or not. During the application for the L/C, the bank may request a deposit or mortgage from the importer. Opening fees would also be required.

Banks other than the issuing bank, when requested by the issuing bank and the exporter, will provide an additional guarantee for the payment of the L/C. This is called credit confirmation and the bank is called the confirming bank. Generally, the confirming bank is the exporter's notifying bank. The issuing bank will notify the exporter through their branch office in the exporter's country or their correspondent bank. Thus the bank notifying is called a notifying bank or an advising bank. The L/C is transferred from the issuing bank to the notifying bank by the system called SWIFT, which is a telegraph and computer network system. The original is sent by mail later.

In the L/C transaction, the exporter is called a beneficiary because the exporter is the one who will benefit from the L/C payment guarantee. The beneficiary prepares the documentary draft according to the conditions stated in the L/C and submits it to the exporter's bank or the bank appointed by the L/C.

After the bank receives the documentary draft, the bank has to examine it to see whether it matches the conditions stated in the L/C or not. If there is no problem, the bank makes the payment to the beneficiary. The amount to be paid is the face amount of the draft, deducted by the interest until the maturity date. This price deduction is called a negotiation, and the bank that conducts the negotiation is called a negotiating bank. However, instead of negotiation, the beneficiary may use forfeiting. In negotiation, the issuer or the beneficiary needs to return the money to the bank if the opening bank or the applicant refuses payment later for a justified reason; in forfeiting they do not have to return it.

The documentary draft bought from the exporter's negotiating bank is sent to the opening bank or the appointed bank in the nation of the draft currency. Only the draft is sent to the appointed bank if it is a different bank appointed as a drawee. If the payment currency is US Dollar, a bank in New York will be the addressed bank. If the currency is Yen, a bank in Tokyo will be the addressed bank. If the draft is a sight bill, the addressed bank will be called a paying bank since they will pay right after. However, if a term bill is used, the bank will be called as an accepting bank since the bank promises to pay when the time is due.

1-3 Types of L/C

The history of L/C began with traveler's L/C, which is used to avoid the risk of bringing a lot of cash while traveling. However, at present, very few use Traveler's L/C and commercial L/C is more common. Therefore, L/C usually refers to commercial L/C.

In commercial L/C, the most common one is documentary L/C. Documentary L/C is an L/C that requires the exporter to attach the shipping documents as a guarantee in their documentary draft when they issue the bill of exchange. In addition, there is a documentary L/C, which basically requires the exporter to send the shipping documents directly to the importer. This kind of L/C is called documentary clean credit, and is widely used in transaction among company's branches or transaction inside the company.

Clean credit is an L/C that does not require the exporter to attach shipping documents to the draft. This is used for payment by remittance and payment of freight and insurance premium.

In addition to the basic classification of L/C types above, L/C can be classified more specifically into different types. One type of L/C mentioned above can be differentiated into some types of L/C according to the dealings and differences in function.

① Stand-by Credit

Stand-by credit is one type of clean L/C. In this L/C, the exporter does not have to submit the shipping documents or any other guarantee documents to the bank. The payment usually depends on the remittance from the importers to the exporters. If the importer fails to pay the exporter, the issuing bank should guarantee the payment. The issuing bank does not need to wait for the shipping documents submission to guarantee the payment, but the bank must always be prepared for guarantee. This kind of L/C is called stand-by credit.

In order to join an international bid such as plant exports or a major international project, the enterprise should prepare the bid guarantee. In fact, in many cases, the bank issues the Bid Bond for the

Figure 17   Basic category of L/C

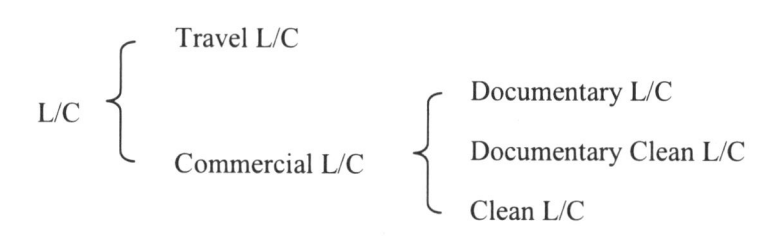

$$L/C \begin{cases} \text{Travel L/C} \\ \text{Commercial L/C} \begin{cases} \text{Documentary L/C} \\ \text{Documentary Clean L/C} \\ \text{Clean L/C} \end{cases} \end{cases}$$

enterprises. This Bid Bond is also a type of stand-by credit. Another type of stand-by credit is the performance bond, which guarantees contract fulfillment of the successful bidder. Moreover, another stand-by credit is the Refund Bond; a guarantee that pays back the advance payment already paid to the exporter if the exporter cannot execute the contract later. This usually occurs in advance payment such as plant or ship construction.

② Irrevocable Credit and Revocable Credit

Irrevocable credit is an L/C which contents cannot be changed or cancelled without the agreement of the issuing bank, the applicant, the beneficiary and all the parties concerned. On the contrary, revocable credit is an L/C that the issuing bank can freely change, revise, or delete the L/C's contents.

③ Confirmed credit and Unconfirmed Credit

Confirmed credit is an L/C which is confirmed by additional banks other than issuing bank. On the other hand, unconfirmed credit is an L/C without additional confirmation from other banks (only guaranteed by an issuing bank).

Unconfirmed credit does not mean that there is a problem in the credit so that it is guaranteed only by the issuing bank. However, confirmed credit is preferred when the credibility of the issuing bank is low or the country risk is high so that the guarantee from the issuing bank will not be secure enough. In that case, the issuing bank or the beneficiary can apply for another confirmation from another banks. In many cases, the advising bank also becomes the confirming bank.

④ Special Credit and General Credit

A documentary draft prepared by the beneficiary is commonly negotiated by the exporter's bank. In special credit, the exporter's bank negotiating the documentary draft is appointed. In general credit, there is no appointed bank and any bank can freely negotiate the documentary draft. If the importer does not decide which credit, the issuing bank will decide.

⑤ Revolving Credit

There is a system where an L/C can be used repeatedly in the case of regular transactions of a particular product, in order to save cost and omit the procedure of issuing the L/C for every shipment. This kind of credit is called a revolving credit. The same L/C can be used many times within the effective period and duration.

Since the amount of this kind of credit is a little higher than each transaction amount in most case, there may be an amount unused. This balance is added to the next transaction in cumulative revolving credit. This is a system in which the present amount is added to the next L/C amount. On the other hand, non-cumulative revolving credit is a system in which the remaining balance is not transferred to the next L/C.

⑥ Back to Back Credit

Back to back credit is often used in intermediary trade, where goods bought from one country are resold in other countries. According to the L/C issued by the reseller's bank, the bank in the intermediary country issues the L/C on behalf of the buyer. The conditions of the L/C are the same as the L/C issued by the reseller's bank.

⑦ Deferred Payment Credit.

This is a credit that guarantees payment automatically after the submission of shipping documents to the exporter's bank. There is no need to submit the bill of exchange. Besides the issuance of the bill of exchange and the acceptance, this credit aims to save the revenue tariff.

1-4 Trade Contract and L/C

If the L/C is to be used as the payment method, the importer should apply the issuance of the L/C to their bank. The condition written in the L/C is compiled according to the condition of the contract. In summary, the issuance and the content of the L/C are based on the trade contract.

However, as the L/C is considered as an independent agreement from the trade contract after the issuance of the L/C, the payment is conducted according to the condition of the L/C. This principle is called the L/C's Independent Principle. For example, if a mistake in the L/C is not corrected in the L/C condition, there will be a discrepancy with the L/C although the transaction is executed according to the contract. Sometimes it causes the fault of payment guarantee. In summary, the condition stated in L/C is given priority to the condition in the contract.

In the L/C payment, the exporter should execute the contract according to the condition stated in the contract. When the exporter's bank buys the documentary draft drawn by the exporter, the bank should examine carefully whether the condition in the L/C is the same as the content of the documentary draft. This principle is called the Strict Compliance Principle. However, it is not only about the regulation and definition of the degree of strictness requested. In real practice, we have to pay attention to whether there is a "principle realization" gap among the banks.

The exporter should examine the following points based on the Independence Principal and Strict Compliance Principal. Briefly, the exporter should examine whether there is discrepancy between the L/C and the trade contract, whether the shipment period and L/C period are sufficient, check the payment term and so on. This examination must be conducted immediately after the exporter receives the L/C. If there is a problem or mistake, the exporter should contact the importer and request an L/C amendment. Procedures and practices about L/C are regulated by the Uniform Customs and Practice for Documentary Credits of the ICC.

1-5 Contents of L/C

In the L/C payment, the exporter should submit the documentary draft according to the L/C term and condition. After receiving the L/C notice, the exporter should examine the contents of the L/C thoroughly. If there is a discrepancy between the L/C and the trade/ sales contract, the exporter has to request an L/C amendment to the importer. Therefore, it is very important to understand the L/C correctly.

The contents of the L/C are based on the standard preparation form of the International Commercial Conference. Therefore there is no big difference between the banks that issue it. The L/C can be issued in a letter draft form or telegraph form. Although most of the L/C is issued in a telegraph form, for the purposes of our study, we will examine and refer to the letter draft form of L/C in this book.

A. Issuing/Opening Bank: The issuing bank is written in the upper right

hand side, outside the column, COMMERCIAL BANK OF HOCHIMINH. The bank's branch name, location, and mailing address are also written.
B. The issuing method: In the first row, before entering the content of the L/C, it is written that the same L/C has been issued by telecommunication. The L/C is first issued by telecommunication and the same contents of the L/C are issued and sent by post.
C. L/C Type: This L/C is irrevocable documentary; the L/C number is 8716; the Date of Issue is January 4, 2001.
D. Applicant: The applicant is PROTRADE Company. The company's address is written below the company name.
E. Advising Bank/Noticing Bank: In the advising bank column, the bank's name, address, and reference number are written. In the sample L/C, the advising bank is THE BANK OF FUKUOKA, HIGASHIMACHI branch.
F. Beneficiary: In the beneficiary column, the beneficiary's name, which is the exporter, is written. In the L/C sample, the beneficiary is KURUME SHINKO Company.
G. Date and Place of Expiry: EXPIRY DATE is the effective period of L/C. In the L/C sample, the expiry date is February 14, 2001. This is the dateline for the beneficiary to request negotiation of the documentary draft by the exporter's bank. It is not the arrival dateline of the documentary draft in the issuing exporter's bank. To confirm this, Place of Expiry, which is Japan, is written.
H. AMOUNT: Amount means the credit amount. The L/C amount is the guaranteed amount, which is the highest amount possible. The credit amount is stated in number which is followed by the alphabetic version. The last word is ONLY.
I. Bill of Exchange Amount: The amount should be the same as the invoice value.
J. Partial Shipment and Transshipment: Partial Shipment is allowed and transshipment is not allowed.

Format 12: Documentary Letter of Credit

COMMERCIAL BANK OF HOCHIMINH
Thuan An Branch
S8U4 Thuan An District, Binh Duong Province, VIETNAM   Cable Address: Cobankhochi

This refers to our preliminary teletransmission advice of this credit

IRREVOCABLE DOCUMENTARY LETTER OF CREDIT No. 8716	APPLICANT PROTRADE P8G3 THUNG AN DISTRICT, BINH DUANG PROVINCE VIETNAM
DATE OF ISSUE: JANUARY 4, 2001	
ADVISING BANK Ref. No. THE BANK OF FUKUOKA, HIGASHIMACHI 3-2-1 HIGASHIMACHI, KURUME, FUKUOKA, JAPAN	BENEFICIARY KURUME SHINKO CO., INC. 3-4-5 HIGASHIMACHI KURUME, FUKUOKA, JAPAN
DATE AND PLACE OF EXPIRY FEBRUARY 14, 2001 JAPAN	AMOUNT JP¥1,440,000 (JAPANESE YEN ONE MILLION FOUR HUNDRED AND FORTY THOUSAND ONLY)

Covering   100   % invoice value.

Partial Shipments: (X) allowed ( ) not allowed   Transhipments: ( ) allowed (X) not allowed

Shipment / dispatch / taking in charge from / at HAKATA PORT   SHIPMENTS LATEST: JANUARY 31, 2001 for transportation to HOCHIMINH PORT, VIETNAM

Credit Available with   ANY BANK   by negotiation against presentation of the documents detailed below and your draft(s) at ··············· sight drawn on THE COMMERCIAL BANK OF HOCHIMINH, THUANG AN, VIETNAM

MERCHANDISE DESCRIPTION:

SHINKO BOND E-20210
JP¥1,440,000 CIF HOCHIMINH

DOCUMENTS REQUIRED:
1. SIGNED COMMERCIAL INVOICE IN TRIPLICATE
2. MARINE INSURANCE POLICY OR CERTIFICATE FOR 110% OF INVOICE AMOUNT AGAINST ALL RISKS INCLUDING WAR & S.R.C.C. RISKS IN DUPLICATE
3. FULL SET CLEAN OCEAN BILLS OF LADING MADE OUT "TO ORDER OF SHIPPER" BLANK ENDORSED AND MARKED "FREIGHT PREPAID" AND "NOTIFY ABOVE APPLICANT"
4. PACKING LIST IN DUPLICATE

Documents to be presented within   10   days after the date of issuance of the shipping documents but within the expiry of the credit

We hereby issue this Documentary Credit in your favor. It is subject to the Uniform Customs and Practice for Documentary Credits, 1993 revision, ICC Publication No. 500 and engages us in accordance with the terms thereof. The number and the date of the credit and the name of our bank must be quoted on all drafts required. If the credit is available by negotiation, each presentation must be noted on the reverse of this advice by the bank where the credit is available.

All documents to be forwarded in one cover, by airmail, unless otherwise stated above. Negotiating bank charges, if any, are fro account of beneficiary. The advising bank is required to notify the credit to the beneficiary without adding their condition.

This document consists of
1   singed page(s).
           Taro Tamiya Authorized Countersignature | Ngyan Ngoc Lan   Authorized Signature

Please examine this instruction carefully. If you are unable to comply with the terms or conditions, please communicate with your buyer to arrange for an amendment. This procedure will facilitate prompt handling when documents are presented.

K. Place of Delivery and Dateline: This term states when and where the seller delivers the goods to the buyer. In the L/C sample, the goods should be delivered from Hakata Port by the end of January 2001. The destination port is HOCHIMINH Port, Vietnam. However, the L/C deadline is often set two weeks after the delivery/ shipment dateline.

L. Negotiating Bank: Credit available with ANY BANK by negotiation means that there is no special bank appointed to negotiate the documentary draft. This kind of L/C is called general credit. If the negotiating bank is appointed, the name of the bank should be written instead of "ANY BANK.' Shipping documents are presented to fulfill the condition stated in the negotiation. The required shipping documents are written in the next column.

M. The condition of the draft: For 'At sight,' the issuing bank's name should be written in the drawee column. In the L/C payment, most often the issuing bank becomes the drawee.

N. Merchandise Description: the name of the goods transacted and the price are written here.

O. Documents Required: The documents required are documents that should be submitted as shipping documents. For example, there are three copies (triplicate) of commercial invoice and Marine Insurance Policy or Certificate. The insured amount should be 10% higher than the invoice amount. Thus, CIF Amount becomes 10% more. The special contract should be made for the insurance condition, such as ALL RISKS and WAR&SRCC RISKS. Two copies (in duplicate) of the insurance documents should be made.

The Bill of Lading should be issued in full set. The original B/L is usually issued in three copies and the exporter has to give all of the copies. The B/L is used in international freight and is not used in domestic freight. The B/L is issued in the form "TO ORDER OF SHIPPER" and not in "BLANK ENDORSED". If the B/L is FREIGHT PREPAID, "NOTIFY ABOVE APLICANT" should be

written. Finally, three copies of the packing list should be submitted.
P. The deadline for submitting the shipping documents to the negotiating bank is "within the expiry date", but each document should be presented to the bank within ten days after the issuing date. If it is submitted late, it becomes a stale document and cannot be bought.
Q. Sentences starting with, "We hereby issue", explains that if the L/C is issued for the exporter as a beneficiary, it should obey the conditions regulated in The Uniform Customs and Practice for Documentary Credits. This paragraph is called a statement of Uniform Customs and practice for Documentary Credits.
R. The remaining sentences explain the required procedures. As written, the number, the date of the credit and the name of the bank must be quoted on all drafts required. If the credit is available by negotiation, each presentation must be noted on the reverse of the L/C by the bank where the credit is available. All documents are to be forwarded in one cover. The negotiating bank charges account for the beneficiary and the advising bank is required to notify the credit to the beneficiary without adding the condition.
S. In the last column, the number of the pages of noticing documents, name and signature of the noticing bank's person in charge, and name and signature of the issuing bank's person in charge.
T. In the last phrase presented to the beneficiary, they are reminded to examine the credit carefully. If there are some problems, the beneficiary has to communicate with the buyer to make arrangements for amendments.

2 Drawing Bill of Exchange

In L/C payment or documentary collection payment, the exporter has to draw the Bill of Exchange (Draft). The Bill of Exchange is a document that has value; therefore we need to pay close attention to it. The Bill of Exchange consists of two pages and can be obtained from the issuing bank. The format follows the regulation in the issuing countries and the conditions stated in the L/C. The following points are Japanese-based regulation on the Bill of Exchange:

A. The Bill of Exchange's serial number is written after 'No'. The number is arranged by the issuer.
B. The value amount of the draft is written after the word 'for', following the currency used.
C. The issuing date, exporter countries and the bank address are written at the upper left side of the draft. The issuing date should be within the issuing date of the shipping documents and the L/C dateline.
D. The draft deadline is written after the word "at". In the case of the sight bill, we do not need to write anything under the dot line ------.
E. The beneficiary bank's name in the exporter's country is written after the words 'Pay to'. In many cases, the column after 'pay to' is left in the blank space and the beneficiary bank's name is written in the backside of the draft.
F. The value amount of the draft is spelled out in the blank space, under the words, 'the sum of'. If 'about' or 'circa' is written, it means that the amount is 10% more or less from the stated amount.
G. The name of the person who pays is written after the words 'to account for'. In the payment by documentary draft collection, this column is left blank.
H. The issuing bank's name is written after the words, 'drawn under'. The L/C series number is written after the words 'L/C No.' The L/C issuing date is written after the word 'dated.' For payment by documentary draft, it is left blank.

Format 13: Bill of Exchange

```
                    BILL OF EXCHANGE
       No.  J-12345
                                              KURUME, FUBRUARY 15

       For   JP¥1,440,000
              At ----------------------- Sight of this FIRST of Exchange (Second of the same
       tenor and date being unpaid) Pay to The Bank of Fukuoka, Ltd. or order the sum of
       JAPANESE YEN ONE MILLION FOUR HUNDRED AND FORTY THOUSAND ONLY


       Value received and charge the same to account of   PROTRADE, HOCHIMINH, VIETNAM
       Drawn under   THE COMMERCIAL BANK OF VIETNAM, HOCHIMINH
       L/C No. 8710                  dated  JANUARY 10, 2001
                 To  THE COMMERCIAL BANK
                     OF VIETNAM, HOCHIMINH                              Revenue
                     VVIETNAM              KURUME SHINKO CO INC.
                                                                        Stamp
                                                 (signature)
       666-2 a
```

I. The addressed party's name is written after the word 'To'. For L/C payment, the name of the issuing bank is written. For the documentary draft payment, the name of the buyer is written. In the right side, the addressed institution's name is written and also the name of the person in charge.

J. A revenue stamp is required according to Japanese regulation.

3 Trade Finance

3-1 Method of Avoiding Insolvency Risk

In payment methods in which the payment will be delivered after the goods are delivered, the seller has to be aware of withdrawal risk. If there is uncertainty on buyer's ability to pay the bill, we have to take action to avoid this risk. Specifically, after the completion of the trade contract, we have to apply for the Bill of Exchange at the bank. In general, there are some methods to avoid the risk, namely the L/C, negotiation, factoring, and the export's insurance. As L/C has been explained previously, here, we will focus on negotiation, factoring, and trade insurance (export's insurance).

Negotiation is a system in which the exporter's bank will pay the bill of exchange to the exporter. Actually, the seller (exporter) cannot receive the payment before the maturity of the draft. However, the seller can receive the payment earlier through negotiation and the interest amount until the maturity is discounted from the face value. In most L/C payments, through negotiation, the seller can get the payment before the issuing bank pays. This is one advantage of L/C. Based on the exporter's credibility, negotiation also can be conducted in documentary collection and open account and so on.

Negotiation can be classified into two types: negotiation with recourse and without recourse. In negotiation with recourse, if for some reasons the issuing bank and the buyer fail to pay, the negotiating bank will request the buyer to make the payment. On the other hand, in negotiation without recourse, the negotiation bank has no right to make the payment request. Negotiation without recourse is also known as forfeiting.

Factoring is a form of credit transfer where the seller gets the right to receive payment from the buyer and have credit at the same time. The seller has guaranteed to receive payment by having the right to transfer the credit owned. A company doing factoring is called a factor. Factoring is used in payment without L/C.

The detail is explained below. Before concluding the trade contract, the seller has to complete the factoring contract with the factor. Based on this basic contract, after concluding the trade contract one by one, the seller contacts the bank to apply for factoring. After that, the credit is transferred and the seller receives payment. The seller also has to pay the guarantee fee to the factor. The bank can become the factor itself or become the factor on behalf of another subsidiary company.

Another system to secure trade is the export's bill insurance. It is a system without L/C to give better security to the negotiation bank from loss. By using this system, the bank will buy the bill of exchange issued by the exporter, thus avoiding withdrawal risk.

3-2 Trade Finance
3-2-1 Export Finance
For the exporter, if they can avoid the withdrawal risk by L/C, negotiation, or forfeiting, they do not need to use the export's loan. However, there is a pre-export loan system, which is a system to bear all the costs needed before the shipment, such as production cost, processing cost, cargo, etc.

The pre-export loan system is a system where the bank gives a loan to the exporter or manufacturer appointed by the exporter to fund the cost of production, processing, cargo and so on. In this system, there are two types of loans: loan for L/C payment and non-L/C payment. The required condition for this system is the completion of the export contract.

3-2-2 Import Finance
The main point of import finance is the postponement of the importer's payment by some methods. This is known as the importer usance method, namely bank's acceptance, loan, supplier's credit, and so on.

Foreign bank's acceptance is utilized when the L/C uses a foreign currency term draft. A term draft issued by the exporter is sent to the central bank that has a foreign bill of exchange market. Therefore, the importer's payment is postponed until the dateline of the draft.

For domestic loan, we can use L/C or without L/C. For the draft, we can use sight bill or term draft. When the importer uses the sight bill or term draft/ bill, the domestic bank can lend domestic currency or foreign currency. Then, the importer makes payment to the bill according to the currency.

The supplier's credit is a kind of usance offered by the exporter.

The importer's payment is postponed for a term determined according to the condition of the trade contract. For example, in payment without L/C such as D/A payment and long-term open account payment, the importer's payment is postponed until the payment dateline set. Thus, this system works in the same way as the loan system.

4   Avoiding Foreign Exchange Risk

4-1   Foreign Exchange Risk

Foreign exchange risk is a risk or loss because of foreign exchange rate fluctuation. This fluctuation causes, for example, failure to get the estimated interest or the estimated payment amount. There is loss because rate fluctuation is known as an exchange loss.

Trade transaction is not an advanced payment transaction; therefore, there is a time gap between the conclusion of the contract and payment. Moreover, both the foreign exchange and domestic exchange are subject to market price speculation. Therefore, both the exporter and importer have to be aware of foreign fluctuation risk.

For example, goods that have a value of ¥1,000,000 are exported. It is offered to the partner in dollars, which is US$5,000 (rate 1 dollar = 200 Yen). However, at the time of payment, the rate of a dollar becomes 100 Yen, and therefore we can get a payment of only ¥500,000. On the contrary, when we import goods priced at $5,000 Based on the contract, we plan to pay ¥1,000,000, but at the time of payment, we only have to pay ¥500,000 Yen. Based on the above example, from the exporter side, if the rate has increased, we receive less money. If the Yen becomes cheaper, we do not need to pay as much as we estimated. From the importer side, it works in the opposite way.

Therefore, there is a possibility that we can get some profit gain from exchange's fluctuation. In other words, the risk is sometimes profitable and we do not always need to take some risk's prevention policy. If we want to take some risk's prevention policy, we always have to consider about the cost and foreign exchange rate. Also, although we hedge the risk, we still do not know whether it will secure the entire payment amount or only part of it.

4-2 Avoiding Foreign Exchange Risk
4-2-1 Forward Exchange Contract

Foreign exchange risk occurs because of the gap in rate at the time of the contract and payment. Therefore, if possible, the exchange rate at the time of the contract becomes the rate at the time of payment. This is a basic concept of the forward exchange contract.

Exchange transaction consists of two types, namely the spot exchange contract and forward exchange contract. In the spot exchange contract, the real exchange is within two days after the transaction contract. In the forward exchange contract, the actual exchange is two days after the transaction contract.

The exchange contract can be classified as the selling contract (the bank sells the exchange) and the buying contract (the bank buys the exchange). The selling contract is for import transaction and the buying contract is for export transaction.

In the exchange contract, after the conclusion of the contract, bank has to refer daily to the official announcement of the forward exchange rate. According to the spot rate in the foreign exchange market, the bank will calculate the forward rate and offers it to the buyer. By using the forward exchange rate, the exporter does not need to estimate the export's price and can write the price in their currency. Later, the importer uses the forward rate to calculate the price in domestic currency and does not need to compute the domestic's current price.

The forward rate offered by the bank is based on the foreign exchange market rate reconciliation at 10 a.m., which is then added by the bank's transaction cost or Telegraphic Transfer Selling Rate (TTS Rate) and Telegraphic Transfer Buying Rate (TTB Rate). The delivery condition in the exchange contract's transaction uses the Calendar Month Delivery with Option. The delivery time is the month after the decided month and can be delivered within one month from the 1st to the 30th/ 31st.

To apply for exchange contract, we have to submit the contract slip to the bank. The documents needed for application are buying contract slip for export, the selling contract slip for import, the foreign currency document, contracted rate, fulfillment period, and so on.

When the time comes, the exporter and the importer present the contract slip and apply to the bank to execute the contract. Fulfillment of the contract means fulfillment of the exchange trade at the contracted price amount. However, because the contracted rate is a telegraphic transfer rate without interest, its interest is calculated based on exchange term and payment condition. In a forward exchange contract, the contract must be executed even though the trade contract is cancelled. Therefore, in the buying contract, we have to get the exchange currency on the spot, present it to the bank and ask the bank to execute the contract. In the selling contract, the bank presents the bill of exchange and we buy it.

Nowadays, the contract is not only for a particular rate contract, but we can also make a range rate. We can execute the contract within the profitable rate. This system is known as a range forward. Another system is the knockout forward. In this system, the contract will be cancelled if the expected rate is exceeded, or depending on the enterprises, there is a comprehensive contract for all transactions during a span of some years.

4-2-2 Currency Option

After the completion of the forward exchange contract, we cannot cancel the contract no matter how much profit or loss there is. The exchange contract is a duty; a method to get the right of fulfillment of the contract even by premium. This is called as currency option; this kind of premium is known as an option premium. The currency option for importer is put option and call option for the exporter. The option is a right which we can compare with the contracted rate and spot rate at the time of contract fulfillment. If the spot rate is more profitable, we can cancel the contract and transact the exchange at the spot rate.

4-2-3   Quotation in Yen

From Japan's perspective, if we do a transaction using a foreign currency, it will be subject to the market fluctuation's risk. Therefore, by using Yen in trade transaction, we can avoid this risk and the other country has to bear the risk. Yen is often used in trade transaction between Asian countries. In world trade, the dollar is more common. Moreover, in the international market, the price of the goods is mostly stated in US Dollars.

4-2-4   Estimation of Yen Appreciation and Depreciation

Based on the real rate, in export, the yen tends to appreciate and in import, the yen tends to depreciate. By using the exchange's fluctuation range, we can expect wider fluctuation risk estimation. However, either in export and import, the estimation is higher that the estimated real rate price and it causes a lack of competitiveness. In fact, the export or import of a big enterprise is in a competitive environment and they have estimation for appreciation as well as depreciation.

4-2-5   Exchange Marry

Buying exchange in export's payment and selling exchange in import's payment are closely related. For example, if a currency fluctuates and causes loss in the buying exchange, it is also causes gain in the selling exchange. On the contrary, if the selling exchange is gaining, the buying exchange is losing. Therefore, if in the same day, a company makes payment at the same price for buying exchange and selling exchange, the loss and gain for those transactions will offset each other. This hedging risk method is known as Exchange Marry.

In fact, there is a very small possibility that the price of buying and selling exchange will be the same. Therefore, to cope with the price gap between the buying and selling contract, we consider other methods. For example, the currency we bought is deposited to the bank, and we receive the payment on another day; thus, there is no need to buy and sell at the same price.

4-2-6　Netting

If both of the trade parties both export and import to each other, it can offset the payment amount and the amount received by the parties, and thus avoiding exchange risk. This kind of method, which both parties can offset debt and credit each other, is known as netting. By this method, we can avoid exchange risk, and at the same time, we can save the transaction cost paid to the bank.

　　There are two types of netting, namely bilateral netting, which is netting between two parties, and multilateral netting, which is netting among more than three parties.

4-2-7　Leads and Lags

If we talk about the foreign exchange market place, making payment earlier or later is called leads and lags. If we expect yen appreciation, the exporter should ask for an advanced payment by making the payment dateline earlier in order to get the yen earlier. On the contrary, if the importer is late in completing the contract and the payment is late, then there is a possibility to gain more. If we expect yen depreciation, the exporter can receive the payment late and have possibility to gain more; the importer has to make the payment earlier to avoid further loss.

4-2-8　Foreign Currency Loan

It is possible to get a loan according to the currency used. For example, at completion of the contract, the exporter receives the payment from the bank and borrows the same amount of money with the payment in foreign currency, and exchanges it to Yen. At the time of payment, we give back the money borrowed from the bank, using the payment that we received from the bank. In the case of import, after the completion of the contract, the importer borrows money in yen, exchanges it to the foreign currency, and deposits it. After that, they can make a payment in that foreign currency.

Questions

1 Explain the relationship between L/C and sales contract
2 Explain about trade finance, methods of avoiding withdrawal risk, and trade loan.
3 Discuss in class why it is said that the more internationalized an enterprise is, the lower its risk will be on foreign exchange.
4 As the L/C is used less, it becomes more common for the banks at the exporter's place to directly finance the exporters. Explain this process of change.

Part 3 Contract Fulfillment

/ Chapter 1
Export Customs Entry and Shipping

Summary

Export customs entry and shipping procedure will be explained here. We will focus on the preparation of transportation to customs clearance, and the flow of the shipping procedure according to the transportation means. In addition, the method of how the bonded system and the forwarder works in Japan will also be explained.

1 Export Customs Entry Procedure

1-1 Preparation before Transport

The exporter should inspect the item to see if it matches the contract, before putting it on the distribution route. Occasionally, the importer does the quality inspection. Moreover, it is necessary to obtain the necessary certificate of quality when a special inspection has been decided in the contract.

When the inspection is completed, the goods are packed. There are four kinds of packing: packaging that protects each item, interior packing that puts some items together, exterior packing for the entire cargo and bulk cargo that does not pack at all.

It is necessary to stencil or affix shipping marks on the surface of the packing. Shipping marks are used to distinguish one item from another, which is important when the freight reaches the destination before the owner arrives. Care marks are stenciled or affixed according to the character of the freight, such as "fragile", "this side up", "handle with care", "perishable" and so on. The forwarder does not have international transportation modes but prepares all necessary procedures for international transportation.

1-2 Bonded Area Entry and Measurement

The export cargo is transported from a domestic warehouse to the port of embarkation, and is carried into the bonded area. It is a place where the foreign freight can be kept. In principle, the freight must be moved into the bonded-area when an export customs entry or import customs entry is proceeding. There are five kinds of bonded areas in Japan due to the different functions: designated bonded area, bond warehouse, bonded factory, bonded exposition, and integrated bonded area.

The designated bonded area is an area designated by the Minister of Finance, which is managed by the government, the local public organization or corporation that manages the harbors or airport. The bonded area where the chief of customs permits is called the bonded warehouse that is used to clear goods through the customs and to load. The bonded factory aims at the processing trade development of Japan. The bonded exposition is designed to display foreign commodities, such as International Trade Fair, an exhibition of foreign commodities.

The integrated bonded area possesses all functions of the designated bonded area, bond warehouse, bonded factory and bonded exposition. This region aims at the import promotion and is set up as a foreign access zone where the facilities related to the import in harbors, the airport, and the surrounding areas are integrated. In principle, the foreign freight cannot be kept besides the bonded area. However, it is possible to transport the foreign freight between bonded areas that the chief of customs has designated. It is called bonded transportation.

It is necessary to follow the procedures for shipping and customs clearance after the cargo is carried into the bonded area. The forwarder can accomplish both. The sworn measure measures the cargo at the bonded area before shipping and customs clearance. The measurement results are filled into the shipping order, the mate's receipt, and the B/L, which becomes the basic material for fare calculation. If necessary, shipping documents, the Certificate and the List of Measurement and/or Weight are issued at this stage. In airline transportation, the air cargo agency carries out this measurement.

1-3 Export Customs Entry
1-3-1 Export Customs Entry Procedure
When export goods are carried into the bonded area, the customs clearance procedure should be done. As a rule, the cargo shipment can be made only after customs clearance is completed and the export permission is acquired. The forwarder executes customs clearance as a customs broker.

You must prepare the export declaration, the commercial invoice, and export license if necessary. Some domestic consumption taxes, such as tobacco and alcohol taxes are exempted.

Customs clearance declaration is done by Nippon Automated Cargo Clearance System (NACCS) through the computer network.

The customs house examines the above documents according to tariff method and related laws. This is called documentary inspection. The export articles may be inspected if necessary. This is called spot inspection. After the documentary examination or item inspection, if there is no problem for declaration, and it is considered lawful, a permission signature is given to the export declaration and returned to the customs broker. It is export permit. Now in NACCS this procedure is replaced with the output of the input data from the computer system.

1-3-2 Other Export Customs Entry Procedures
Here, reshipment and modification on export will be explained. Foreign freight are temporarily kept in the bonded area, and then reshipped to the foreign countries in a bond state. This situation is called a reshipment. When the reshipment is taken, the title of export permit certificate should be changed into reshipment. Others are the same as export customs declaration.

If it is necessary to make changes in the export permit or cancel it after the export clearance procedure has been completed, the procedure to cancel the export should be carried out. If it is necessary to cancel the export when the customs clearance procedure is being taken, the export declaration withdrawal application is to be submitted.

After acquiring an export permit, if the export is cancelled due to the abandonment of voyage or cancellation of the export contract, the cancellation of export procedures should be taken. Once the export permit is acquired, an import declaration is necessary to cancel export. It is necessary to follow the import customs entry procedure when the cargo is loaded onto the vessel or aircraft. If the cargo has not been loaded yet, you can make a simplified declaration by attaching the export permit to the import declaration. Both cases are exempted from the tariff. If any modification is made to the quantity or loading ship after acquiring the export permit, a submission of change application attached to the export permit is required.

1-3-3 Special Export Customs Entry Procedures

The following customs clearance procedures are applied when it is difficult to proceed with the normal customs clearance procedure.

A. Export declaration for the mother ship before being carried into the bonded area

Normally, an export declaration can be made only if the cargo has been carried into the bonded area. However, if there is no consolidated cargo in the mother ship, it is possible to make the export declaration without it being carried into the bonded area. Moreover, this rule can be applied to perishable foods, flora and fauna as well.

B. Container Vanning

In principle, the container cargo needs an export declaration before loading. However, to save time, if an application of container loading is made in advance, the container cargo can make an export declaration. This is called inclusive pre-examination system.

C. Air Cargo

Air cargo is speedy. The export declaration by the air cargo simplicity export declaration book is admitted.

D. ATA Carnet Customs Clearance

Temporarily exporting goods that will be returned to the exporting country later, as well as occupational tools, exhibit, and sample commodities can clear export and import customs by the customs clearance book according to the ATA Carnet. The ATA Carnet is based on the ATA treaty.

E. Special Export for Sea Food

Domestic fishing boats require qualification of foreign trade vessel in order to export sea food that are captured in the open sea, directly to foreign countries. There is no inspection for these goods. The export declaration can be sent to the headquarters by telecommunication.

F. Temporary Opening and Off-Time Work

If the customs clearance procedure is taking place during customs off-job time, it is called temporary opening. The importer or exporter has to take some necessary procedures in order to make the customs clearance, such as loading cargo and unloading cargo.

G. Others

The simple way of customs clearance can be done for the following goods: cargo which is less than ¥200,000, container, mail, equipment for vessel or aircraft, carrying goods and so on.

2 Shipping Procedure

2-1 Marine Transport

Most sea transportation is done by container vessel. As explained previously, container cargo is divided into FCL and LCL.

FCL cargo, which fills one container, needs to submit an equipment receipt when a container is taken from the container yard. Then, the forwarders load the cargo in the forwarder's bonded warehouse or the exporter's warehouse onto the container that was borrowed from the container yard. This is called shipper's pack. Then, the forwarders as a customs broker clear the customs. After acquiring the export permit, the container cargo should be moved into the container yard together with the container load plan and dock receipt. The container yard's gate clerk examines the submitted documents and checks the externals of the container. The container yard operator issues a signed dock receipt if there is no abnormality. Any problems with the submitted documents or container's externals must be described in the exception section of the dock receipt.

After the export customs entry, the LCL cargo should be moved into CFS (Container Freight Station) together with the export permit and dock receipt. The CFS operator issues a signed dock receipt to the forwarders after checking the submitted documents and inspecting the cargo. Different LCL cargos are consolidated into one container called Carrier's Pack. Forwarders also can make the consolidation themselves at their own warehouse. If there is any abnormality in any cargo in the container, it should be described in the transport documents.

The forwarder submits the export permit attached with a signed dock receipt to the shipping company. The shipping company issues the B/L based on these documents. Once the shipping company receives the cargo, the container B/L is issued. However, it is not the certificate of shipment. In the letter of credit payment, the bank rejects a received B/L. Therefore, the shipping date should be confirmed and signed. This is called on board notation.

2-2   Air Transport

Air cargo is divided into direct cargo and consolidated cargo. Direct cargo is when the shipper requests transportation directly to the airline. Direct cargo is mostly applied to large cargo. The bigger it is, the more advantages there are for the transportation fare per kilo. The consolidator makes the consolidated cargo between the shippers and the airlines. The consolidator collects the small cargos from the different shippers and makes the consolidated cargo. Then, the consolidator requests air transportation to the airline. Most international air cargo is consolidated cargo since it is mostly small-sized.

    Direct cargo is when the shipper's request air transportation directly through the air cargo agent and makes a contract with airlines. The air cargo agent collects cargo from the shipper's warehouse and carries it to the international airport and a nearby bonded warehouse. For example, TACT (Tokyo Air Cargo Terminal) and OACT (Osaka Air Cargo Terminal) are places next to international airports where customs clearance and air cargo loading take place. Customs clearance takes place in the bonded warehouse and the air cargo containers are loaded into the aircraft.

    After collecting the cargo, the air cargo agent should issue an air waybill to the shipper before loading it onto the aircraft. The consolidator plays the role of a contracting carrier for the shippers and requests air transportation to the airlines (actual carrier). In this case, there is no big difference between direct cargo and consolidated cargo. The consolidator issues an air waybill to the shippers and the airlines issues an air waybill to the consolidators. The former is called house air waybill and the latter is called master air waybill.

3 Shipping Advice

After making the shipment, the exporter needs to send shipping advice to the importer. Shipping advice informs the importer about the type and quantity of the cargo, the means of transport, the departure date and arrival date so that the importer will be able to arrange for a marine insurance policy and take the cargo. According to Incoterms provisions, one of the exporter's obligations is to send shipping advice. If necessary, a shipping sample or advance sample is sent to clarify the quality of the cargo or to prompt import customs entry.

Questions

1 Explain briefly about export customs entry procedure
2 Explain the shipment of air transport and marine transport.
3 Summarize the forwarder's function and discuss problems in regard to trade transaction.

Chapter 2
Trade Payment

Summary

After completing the shipment of the goods, the exporter proceeds to the payment procedure based on the payment method agreed on in the contract. The exporter has to prepare the documentary draft. In this chapter, we would like to discuss the documents required to prepare the documentary draft. The formation and delivery of the draft are discussed in other chapters. First, we would like to discuss the methods in details, from the perspective of the foreign exchange market, and export payment and import payment, such as open account, L/C, and documentary draft.

1   Preparation of Documentary Bill of Exchange (Draft)

The exporter proceeds with the payment procedure and prepares for the Documentary Bill of Exchange/ Documentary Draft. The documentary draft consists of bill of exchange and shipping documents. The shipping documents consist of some major documents such as the commercial invoice, the bill of lading, the air way bill and other transport documents, including an insurance policy if the exporter had applied for it. Commercial invoice and transport documents are especially needed. The attached documents are a packing list, certificate and list of measurement and/or weight, certificate of origin, some inspection certificates, and a certificate of pre-shipment inspection and so on. Below, we will explain each document briefly. For more detailed information, please refer to the appropriate documents.

A commercial invoice is a document prepared by the exporter, explaining the units, the size, and price of the goods. It is used for customs clearance and must be made according to the domestic customs clearance law. If it includes freight details, it works as a payment request.

A transport document is a certificate for proceeding with the freight shipment and the delivery to the carrier. It includes documents such as the bill of lading, the air waybill, the sea waybill, and the combined transport document. The bill of lading and multimodal shipping documents are generally issued as a document of title, but the sea waybill and the air waybill are not documents of title.

The insurance policy is a testimony document of cargo insurance. Sometimes, a certificate of insurance is issued. If there is no need to apply for insurance, the exporter does not need to submit the insurance policy. It depends on the trade terms. Issuing insurance policy is one of the exporter's obligations only in the case of CIF or CIP.

The packing list is a document explaining the cargo size, units, contents, and so on. It is sent as an additional document to the commercial invoice.

The certificate and list of measurement and/or weight is a certificate the measurement and weight of shipped cargo. A marine inspection company inspects the cargo before shipment. It is basically used for freight calculation. A certificate of origin is a document explaining the country of origin, where the goods are produced or manufactured. It is issued by the chamber of commerce and industry or other designated organizations. It is a very important document to decide which appropriate tariff should be applied, including the application of preferential tariff and import restriction. The inspection certificate is a document explaining the quality and cost of the goods. Official inspection institutions conduct inspection and issues certificates. Sometimes, however, the manufacturer of the cargo conducts inspection and issues the certificate. The certificate of pre-shipment inspection is a document explaining the result of inspection on the goods' price, unit, and so on. Some developing countries require this document for customs clearance. Inspection companies or official agents will conduct inspection and issue the certificate.

The bill of exchange attached to the shipping documents is called a documentary draft. It is rationale that payment is based on the bill of exchange with documents bonding the cargo. Recently, the sea waybill and the air waybill are widely used. However, both bills are not document of title. Therefore, it is still debated whether or not these kinds of payment can be called a documentary draft.

Moreover, in an open account payment, we do not use the bill of exchange. The exporter sends only the shipping document.

Figure 18　Content of Documentary Bill of Exchange

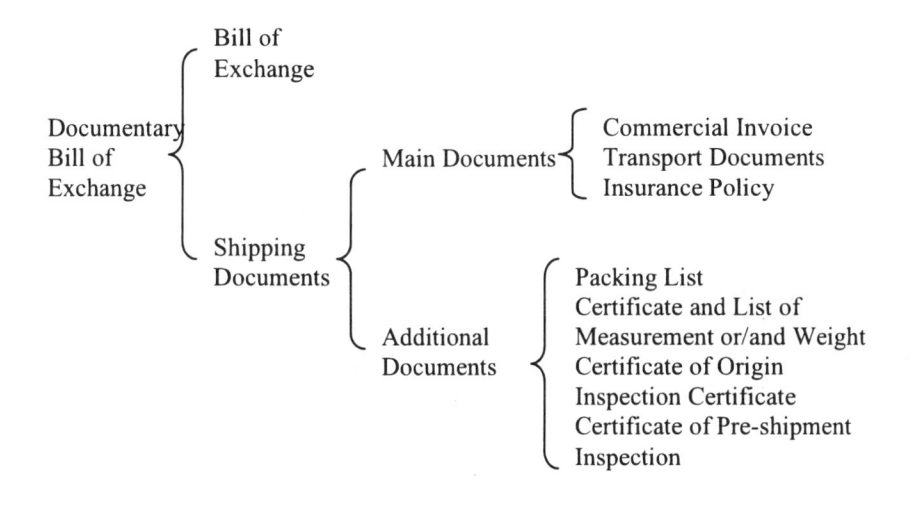

```
                    ┌ Bill of
                    │ Exchange
                    │
Documentary         │                     ┌ Commercial Invoice
Bill of       ─────┤         Main Documents ─┤ Transport Documents
Exchange            │                     └ Insurance Policy
                    │
                    │
                    └ Shipping ─┐
                      Documents │                 ┌ Packing List
                                │                 │ Certificate and List of
                                └ Additional      │ Measurement or/and Weight
                                  Documents      ─┤ Certificate of Origin
                                                  │ Inspection Certificate
                                                  │ Certificate of Pre-shipment
                                                  └ Inspection
```

2 How to Read the List of Exchange Rate

In the case of payment by foreign currency such as dollars or euro, we have to pay close attention to the yen's exchange rate. Here, we will learn how to read the exchange rate that the bank applies to the customer by taking the dollar rate as an example.

In Figure 19, there are seven kinds of rates toward US dollars, which is from TTS to CASH B. In principle, the rate is renewed everyday. If the rate fluctuates above the decided level, it is renewed within one day. From TTS to CASH S. are the rates for the importer and from TTB to CASH B. are the rates for the exporter.

Figure 19   List of Foreign Exchange Rate

	Currency	TTS	ACC.	CASH S.	TTB	A/S	CASH B.
001	USD (US dollar)	104.96	105.14	106.76	102.96	102.78	100.96
002	GBP (Poundsterling)	197.04	197.62	205.04	189.04	188.46	181.04
004	CAD (Canada Dollar)	81.15	81.32	88.15	77.95	77.78	70.95
005	CHF (Swiss)	83.15	83.28	87.15	81.35	81.22	77.35
007	SEK (Sweden Crone)	14.33	14.37	16.33	13.53	13.49	11.53
020	EUR (Euro)	129.98	130.26	135.98	126.98	126.7	120.98

		FORWARD RATES INDICATION (T.T.)			
	SELL/BUY	1 MONTH	2 MONTH	3 MONTH	4 MONTH
USD	SELLING	104.87	104.77	104.68	104.39
	BUYING	102.81	102.70	102.60	102.25
GBP	SELLING	196.50	195.70	195.10	193.00
	BUYING	188.00	187.30	186.50	184.30
EUR	SELLING	129.75	129.52	129.32	128.73
	BUYING	126.60	126.35	126.13	125.40

These market rates are computed based on the foreign exchange market's rate at 10 a.m. on the day. In the exchange market, the selling rate and buying rate are shown as examples: 104.43~104.14 yen, the selling rate is 104.43 yen, and the buying rate is 104.14 yen. The middle value of the range rate is called a middle rate. When some charge (in this case one yen) is added to the middle rate, it is called TTS rate (Telegraphic Transfer Selling Rate). Also, the middle rate that is subtracted (in this case one yen) is called TTB rate (Telegraphic Transfer Buying Rate). TTS and TTB are the basis of rate that the bank applies to the customer. The other rates are calculated by adding interest rates to TTS and TTB. Details of each rate will be explained along the explanation of payment methods.

Figure 19 also shows a list of the forward rate. We refer to this forward rate when we prepare the forward exchange contract to avoid exchange rate's fluctuation risk. However, in the TT rate for buying and selling, the interest is not yet included. Therefore, the required interest is added at the time of payment.

3   Open Account Payment

An open account payment is a payment method by remittance of the importer. After shipping the cargo, the required shipping documents are prepared and sent to the importer. The exporter does not draw a bill of exchange.

After the importer receives the shipping documents, the importer remits payment to the appointed bank account of the exporter within the deadline of payment that is agreed on in the contract.

When the payment is in dollars, the importer sends a dollar remittance draft and the yen-dollar exchange rate is TTS rate. Later, if the exporter is Japanese, he/ she will exchange the dollar remittance draft to yen at TTB rate.

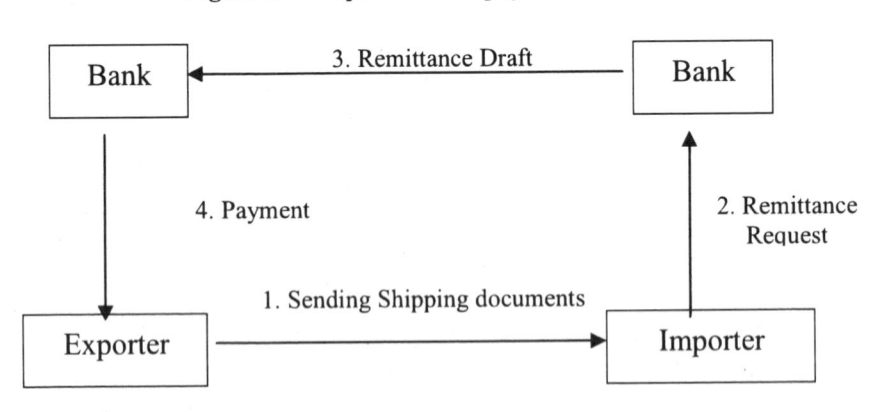

Figure 20   Open Account payment Process

```
┌─────────┐  3. Remittance Draft  ┌─────────┐
│  Bank   │◄──────────────────────│  Bank   │
└─────────┘                       └─────────┘
     │                                 ▲
     │ 4. Payment          2. Remittance Request
     ▼                                 │
┌─────────┐ 1. Sending Shipping documents ┌─────────┐
│ Exporter│──────────────────────────────►│ Importer│
└─────────┘                                └─────────┘
```

Even in an open account payment, if the export's credibility is high, he/ she can apply for trade finance, such as negotiation, forfeiting, factoring, and so on.

4   Payment by Documentary L/C

4-1   Export Payment

The exporter attaches the L/C received from the importer to the documentary draft and contacts the negotiating bank or any bank appointed by the L/C to request a bill of exchange negotiation. In order to do the negotiation, the documentary draft should be presented to the exporter's bank within the period stated in the L/C or before the L/C expiry. However, based on the Uniform Customs and Practice for Documentary Credits, even if the documentary draft is submitted within the L/C period, it is a stale document and cannot be bought if it is more than 21 days after the transport document's date.

The bank receiving the negotiation request should examine the documentary draft based on the condition of the L/C. If there are no problems, then the negotiation will be executed. Negotiation is a form of buying something on behalf of the other party, which later will pay back the amount. Originally, the exporter cannot collect the payment until the documentary draft is sent from the exporter's bank to the importer's bank, and until the importer makes payment. Therefore, the exporter has to bear interest until the payment is received. In summary, it is a draft discount. If the bill of exchange is a sight bill, the foreign exchange rate is A/S rate (At Sight). If it is a term draft, the rate is computed according to each term/ period.

Figure 21   Payment Process by Sight Bill with L/C

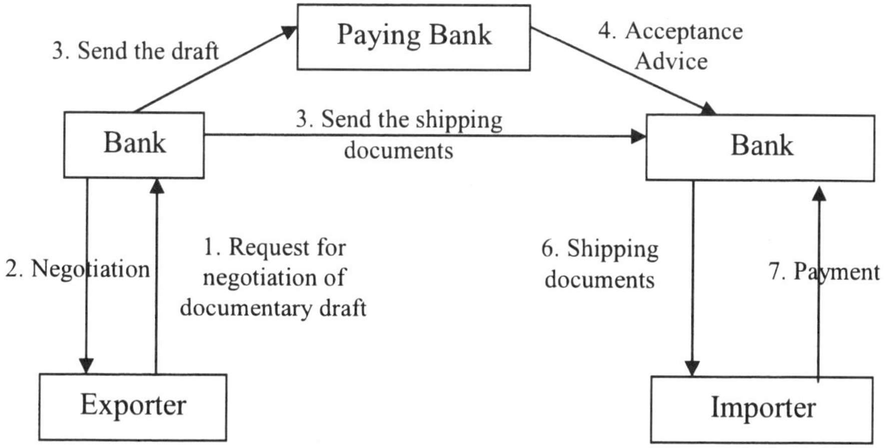

```
                    ┌─────────────┐
         3. Send    │ Paying Bank │    4. Acceptance
         the draft  └─────────────┘       Advice
    ┌──────┐   3. Send the shipping    ┌──────┐
    │ Bank │ ─────documents──────────→ │ Bank │
    └──────┘                           └──────┘
       ↕       1. Request for            ↕
  2. Negotiation  negotiation of    6. Shipping   7. Payment
                documentary draft    documents
    ┌──────────┐                        ┌──────────┐
    │ Exporter │                        │ Importer │
    └──────────┘                        └──────────┘
```

The documentary draft should be examined to see whether it matches the condition stated in the L/C. If there is a discrepancy, disposition should be conducted according to the degree of discrepancy. For example, if the discrepancy is not really serious, the negotiation still can be executed by submitting a letter of guarantee to the exporter. This is called L/G negotiation. Another buying method is by inquiring the importer's bank about the good points and bad points of the

150 Part 3 Contract Fulfillment

negotiation. This is called cable negotiation.

In Japan's negotiation system, there is a right of recourse in the bank. Therefore, if the L/C issuing bank or the importer refuses to make the payment, the exporter has to give back the negotiation amount received. However, if the exporter has high credibility, it is possible to forfeit or negotiation without recourse.

4-2 Import Payment

The exporter's bank sends the documentary draft from the exporter to the importer's bank. However, the bill of exchange is sent directly to the bank, which has the indicated currency market. For example, the US dollar is sent to New York, the yen to Japan's bank branch or a correspondent bank.

For sight bill, the paying bank sends debit advice, which shows that the payment is credited from the issuing bank's account to the issuing bank. The issuing bank examines the shipping document and if there is no problem, they can request the importer to make the payment.

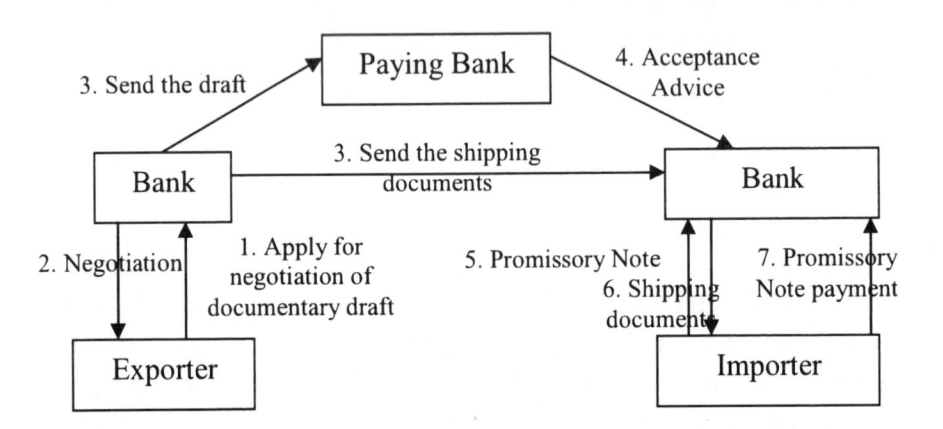

Figure 22 Payment Process of Term Draft with L/C

```
                      ┌─────────────┐
         3. Send the  │ Paying Bank │  4. Acceptance
            draft ──▶ │             │ ◀── Advice
                      └─────────────┘
        ┌──────┐  3. Send the shipping   ┌──────┐
        │ Bank │ ──── documents ───────▶ │ Bank │
        └──────┘                         └──────┘
  2. Negotiation  1. Apply for    5. Promissory Note   7. Promissory
                  negotiation of    6. Shipping        Note payment
                  documentary draft documents
        ┌──────────┐                     ┌──────────┐
        │ Exporter │                     │ Importer │
        └──────────┘                     └──────────┘
```

Then, the importer makes the payment and obtains the shipping documents. The rate accepted as payment rate is called ACC. Rate (Acceptance Rate). This rate is the TTS rate, the payment is credited from the issuing bank's account and interest within the time needed to inform the importer will be added.

If the importer utilizes domestic loan or other trade finance, on the security of the cargo the importer gives trust receipt (T/R), and receives the shipping documents.

The paying bank guarantees the term draft until the time of payment by investing the fund in the market or just maintaining it. The accepting bank sends acceptance advice to the issuing bank. Based on the L/C, the term draft automatically becomes an acceptance method of the foreign bank. The importer, instead of getting the shipping documents, issues a promissory note to promise payment in the draft's maturity date to the issuing bank. The importer has to submit a T/R to the bank. On the draft's maturity date, the money is credited from the issuing bank's account. At the same time, the importer honors the promissory note. In this case, there is no interest and therefore, the applied rate is TTS rate.

5 Payment Documentary Bill of Exchange Collection

This is a payment method by a documentary draft without the L/C. It consists of two methods, namely D/P (documents against payment) and D/A (documents against acceptance).

In both methods, firstly the exporter issues a documentary draft to the bank, and applies for collection. In principle, the documentary draft becomes a bill for collection; the exporter cannot get paid until the importer really makes the payment. If the exporter's credibility is high or the import's draft is insured, bill bought and forfeiting can be conducted. If the issued document is a sight bill, then it is D/P. If it is a term draft, it is D/A.

In D/P method, if the documentary draft arrives at the importer's bank, the importer has to make the payment and then get the shipping documents. If it is in foreign exchange, it will be in TTS rate, and therefore without interest. If using domestic loan, the delivery of shipping documents will be based on T/R.

Figure 23   Process of D/P payment

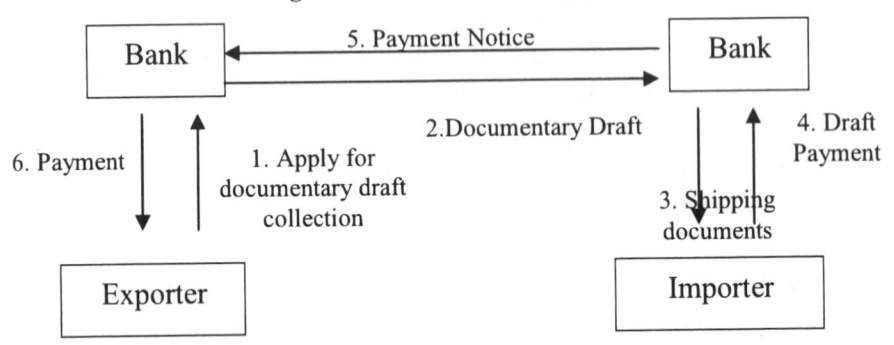

```
        5. Payment Notice
 Bank ◄─────────────────── Bank
   │                         ▲
   ▲                         │
   │     2.Documentary Draft │  4. Draft
6. Payment  1. Apply for     │  Payment
   │     documentary draft   │
   │        collection    3. Shipping
   ▼                       documents
 Exporter                  Importer
```

Figure 24   Process of D/A payment

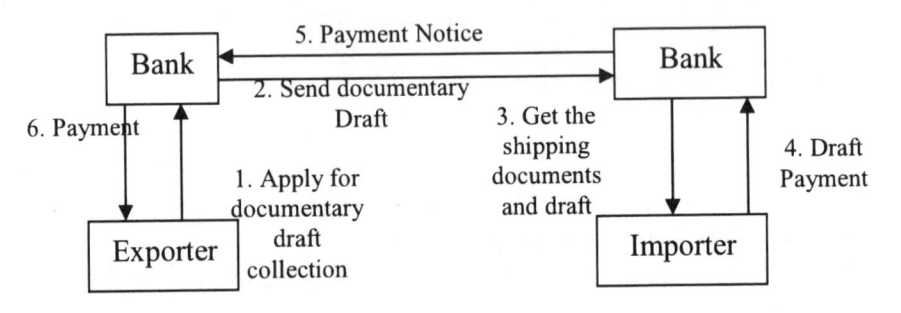

```
        5. Payment Notice
 Bank ◄─────────────────── Bank
   │                         ▲
   ▲   2. Send documentary   │
   │        Draft    3. Get the
6. Payment              shipping    4. Draft
   │     1. Apply for  documents    Payment
   │     documentary   and draft
   │        draft
   ▼     collection
 Exporter                  Importer
```

In D/A method, the importer receives the draft on the draft dateline. Acceptance is a promise to make the payment when the draft dateline comes. The payment clause, payment date, maturity date and institution name are written in the blank space or the back side of the draft. At this point, the importer can get the shipping document. The payment collection is until the draft's dateline. In this case, TTS rate is used, and there is no interest. This method works in the same way as an export's loan; therefore it is also called supplier's credit.

For both D/P and D/A, after the payment is finished, the importer's bank sends the payment and the remittance notice to the exporter bank's account. After the exporter bank receives the notice, they make the payment collection to the exporter. In this case, because there is no rate, the exchange rate is TTB rate.

6 Guarantee Delivery

The importer makes payment of the bill of exchange from the importer's bank, or simply receives the shipping documents by guarantee, exchange B/L and other transport documents to get the cargo. However, due to the speeding up of the ships, the freight can arrive at import ports before the B/L reaches the importer's bank. This is called B/L Crisis, and in this case, we can get the cargo from shipping company by letter of guarantee (double guarantee). This is called delivery of guarantee. After the B/L arrives, the B/L should be submitted, and the letter of guarantee will be returned back to the bank. If there is no joint bank guarantee, a single guarantee is used.

Questions

1 Explain the functions of a documentary draft.
2 Explain T/R
3 It is said that the speeding up of transportation methods underlie the recent shift of payment methods to open accounts. Discuss this causal relationship in class.

Chapter 3
Import Customs Entry and Cargo Receiving

Summary

This chapter discusses the process from the arrival of goods at the import place until the importer receives the goods. Import customs entry, tariff system, unloading of import cargo, insurance claim, and Trade claim are explained in detail. It is especially important that you understand the process from unloading of the cargo to receiving the cargo, the methods of insurance claim, and the resolutions to the sales claim.

1 Import Customs Entry and Tariff System

1-1 Import Customs Entry Procedure

In principle, unloaded cargo should be carried into the bonded area. Then, an import declaration should be made in order to go through customs clearance. The customs broker can make the customs clearance for the cargo. Usually, the customs clearance and cargo receiving procedures are done simultaneously. The cargo cannot be moved out from the bonded area without customs clearance in principle.

The importer needs to attach a commercial invoice, an application for import tariff, in order to make the import declaration; if necessary, the packing list, certificate of origin, import license, tariff Payment book should be attached as well. If the arrival of the shipping documents is later than arrival of the cargo, a proforma invoice can be used for provisional customs clearance. Both import and export customs entry procedures use Air-NACCS and electronic customs clearance system of Sea-NACCS.

Before importing the cargo, ask customs about the tariff rate of the goods that are going to be imported. This is called preliminary instruction system. This system is recommended for new cargo's customs clearance.

Customs examines the documents of the importer's import declaration or the agent's import declaration and if necessary, inspects a sample of the cargo as well. If the result of the import declaration is considered legal, the customs issues an import permit when the importer makes payment through its agent or the Bank of Japan.

Special import customs entry procedures for ship and barge import declaration before moving into the bonded area, container cargo, air cargo, temporary opening, and off-time work are the same as the export customs entry. For the import customs entry, the cargo can be taken away from the bonded area before issuing the import permit. Moreover, the preliminary examination system can be used for perishable foods or cargo when the delivery-date is limited. This system allows the importer to make an import declaration before the cargo arrives.

1-2 Tariff System of Japan

Import duty, consumption tariff, and domestic consumption tariffes for tobacco tariff and liquor tariff needs to be paid for import cargo. The duty can be calculated according to the cargo's price (Ad Valorem Duties) or the cargo's weight (Specific Duties).

Ad valorem duties of Japan are based on the CIF price. The import cargo's CIF price multiplied by its corresponding tariff rate becomes the import cargo's tariff. The CIF price added to the import tariff, and then multiplied by its domestic consumption tariff rate becomes the domestic consumption tariff.

The applied tariff rate is publicized by the customs tariff law

Not every article is displayed in each tariff rate table. Depending on the article, some are displayed in one table, some are displayed in two, and some are displayed in each table. In principle, the tariff rate is applied in the order of the preference tariff rate, the conventional tariff, the provisional tariff, and the basic tariff rate.

There are many other special tariff systems. Among them, let's examine preferential duties and the tariff allocation system.

A preferential duties tariff rate is a tariff rate in the preferential duties system according to the mutual agreement of the United Nations Conference on Trade and Development (UNCTAD) in 1970. This system is made for the economic development of developing countries. When developed countries import articles from developing countries, duty-free or low tariff rate can be applied. For instance, there is an escape clause method for farm products and a ceiling system for mining goods.

The escape clause method can be applied to preference tariff rate. Also, it has no import quota as far as the goods do not attack the same domestic industries. In the ceiling system, preference tariff rate can be applied as far as the added import quantity is less than the predetermined quantity.

The tariff quota system is can only be applied to specific articles. Under certain import quantity, the low tariff rate is applied. However, high tariff rate is applied once the import quantity exceeds it. This system is mostly applied to agricultural products and is introduced as import liberalism while protecting domestic industries.

2 Import Cargo Receiving

2-1 Transportation Means and Cargo Receiving Preparation

Receiving import cargo is divided into piece goods transportation and chartering transportation. A liner is usually used for piece goods transportation, and divided into conventional ship and container ship according to the ship's structure. The importer starts preparing to receive the cargo when he receives the shipping advice and the shipping company's arrival notice.

Air cargo received differently from direct cargo to consolidated cargo. The importer receives the direct cargo's arrival notice from the airlines. In reverse, the importer receives it from the bulk breaking agent for the consolidated cargo.

2-2 Liner Cargo Receiving

B/L is a necessary document for receiving maritime transportation cargo. In the documentary way of payment, the importer makes the payment to the bank and then receives the shipping documents from the bank. When the importer uses trade finance like import usance, the importer deposits the trust receipt to the bank and receives the B/L.

The importer passes the B/L to the forwarder and requests for taking delivery of the cargo. The forwarder makes the payment for all the expenditure to the shipping company and submits the B/L at the same time. Then, the shipping company issues the delivery order. If the cargo arrives before the shipping documents, the bank can issue a letter of guarantee so that the importer will be able to get the delivery order from the shipping company without submitting the B/L. After that, the procedure to receive the cargo from the container yard and container freight station is different.

If it is a full container load cargo, the importer takes the container from the container yard or the shipping company to deliver it to the importer's warehouse after import customs entry. Either way, the delivery order is needed to receive the cargo.

If it is less container load cargo, the importer submits the delivery order and receives the cargo from the container freight station after the customs clearance. If it is a container cargo, the shipping company makes the delivery record at the same time as the delivery.

When there is any problem with the cargo's quantity or the cargo's condition, it should be described in the delivery record. The delivery record is also called a devanning report. If the forwarder made a consolidation for the less container load cargo, then the forwarder should classify the LCL cargo. The importer should get their cargo from the forwarder' or its local agent.

2-3 Charter Cargo Receiving

For receiving cargo based on the chartering contract, the consignees take the cargo privately. For this reason, it is necessary for the consignees to make arrangements for receiving the cargo and to tell their own stevedore in advance.

After the mother ship enters the port, the unloading of the cargo begins when the unloading preparation by the stevedore is completed and the shipping company sends the unloading preparation notice of readiness to the consignee. The cargo boat note is made for each cargo unloading day. It is necessary to describe any damages or discrepancies in the amount of the quantity of the cargo.

After unloading the cargo, the shipping company makes a laydays statement for the consignee; the dispatch money or demurrage can be calculated based on this statement.

2-4 Air Cargo Receiving

As in seaway cargo, it is necessary to get a delivery order in order to receive air cargo. If it is direct air cargo, the consignee exchanges an airway bill with the delivery order from the airline. If it is consolidated air cargo, the consignee exchanges the airway bill with the delivery order through the consolidation sort agent. Based on this delivery order, the consignees are able to receive cargoes from the warehouse.

However, the air waybill is not a document of title. If the bank chooses to use trade finance, such as a letter of credit payment and import usance, the consignee of the airway bill should be the bank. In this case, a Release Order instead of an air waybill received from the airline or the consolidation sort agent can be used to get the delivery order; then the consignee is able to get the cargo.

3   Insurance Claim

3-1   Discovering Damage and Procedure Afterwards

After unloading the import cargo, the importer entrusts the forwarder to check the cargo whether there is any damage or discrepancy in the amount of quantity. If any damage is discovered, the forwarder informs the importer immediately. In other cases, the importer could find a problem with the cargo after opening it at their warehouse. Then the importer needs to deal with it. In the case of FCL cargo, the inspection should take place at the final warehouse because the container is not opened before reaching the final destination.

When the cargo is damaged or lost, the obligations and the procedures the insurant needs to take are written in the claim notice clause of the insurance policy, Article 9 "Bailee Clause" and "Important Clause" of the Institute Cargo Clauses.

If there is any problem, the importer has to describe it in the delivery record first. Moreover, the importer should prevent the cargo damage from aggravating and must inform the shipping company, the insurance company and the exporter of the fact at the same time. At this stage, it is still not clear which party should take the responsibility for the damaged cargo. To reserve the claim for the damage, the importer should issue a notice of damage to each party. The notice of damage to the shipping company is called a preliminary claim and is different from the final claim that is the official claim for the damage.

It is necessary to inspect the original damage level in the presence of the insurance company and the shipping company.

Depending on the level of damage, the problem may be resolved by the concerned parties. If the cargo was damaged extensively, a surveyor is requested to give an official judgment. The surveyor gives the damage survey or hatch survey, if necessary, to the damaged cargo. The hatch survey is to inspect the bulk cargo that was dampened by water or seawater and determines whether the bulk cargo was damaged or not. The survey also investigates the cause of the water that came in as well. Finally, the surveyor issues a survey report to the importer.

3-2   Claim to Exporter and Shipping Company

If the quality of the cargo is defective or there is a deficiency in quantity, as well as damage and loss caused by imperfect wrapping, the importer can make a claim to the exporter. This is called Trade claim. Trade claim must be done in a way that was written in the contract.

Usually, the period and the method of making a claim are written in the contract. The importer issues the notice of damage within the legal period. The importer can make a claim after receiving the survey report, the certificate of inspection and certificate of capacity and weight.

The claims to the shipping company are preliminary claim and final claim. The preliminary claim is to notify the shipping company of the damage or loss and to reserve the right to claim. After receiving the preliminary claim, the shipping company starts investigating the damaged cargo and notifies the importer when the indemnity acceptance has been decided.

Once the importer receives the indemnity acceptance from the shipping company, the importer officially makes a claim on the shipping company. Then, the importer must submit a claim note, a commercial invoice, a copy of the shipping documents, a boat note and a survey report.

For the compensation amount of the shipping company, the application price is determined as the maximum for cargos that apply the affiliated-price fare; for other cargo, the maximum amount is determined by unit or one package's indemnity limitation.

The shipping company investigates the damaged cargo based on a preliminary claim. Immunity can be decided if the B/L's escape clause or captain's protest is applied. In some cases, the responsibility for the shipping company is indefinite and so the shipping company issues a rejecting letter to notify the importer of rejection. If this happens, the importer attaches the rejecting letter and makes a claim on the insurance company for immunity. If the ship encountered stormy weather during the transportation, the ship's captain should report it to the concerned department and accept attestation for the fact. This is called captain's protest which conjectures that the cargo may have been damaged.

3-3   Claim to Insurance Company
3-1-1 Necessity of Claim to Insurer

If the owner of the cargo receives a rejecting letter from the shipping company, the procedure to make a claim to the insurance company has to be taken. Even if the owner continues to make a claim to the shipping company, the procedure to make a claim to the insurance company must be taken due to the loan form payment from the insurance company. The loan form payment is a loan with no interest that is provided by the insurance company to pay insurance to the insurant when the procedure to make a claim to the shipping company or other consigner is taking place. After the insured receives immunity, the remaining loan deducted by the immunity that the insurance company should pay is paid back to the insurance company.

As for the claim to the insurance company, the procedure is different according to the particular average, general average, and total loss. If general average occurs, some cargo becomes a total loss. These losses will be shared by all of the cargo's owners. This kind of shared loss is called a general average.

3-3-2 Claim for Particular Average and Total Loss

If total loss or particular average occurs, the insurant should report it to the insurance company or the claim settling agent according to the important clause written in the insurance policy. The insurance policy, the original insurance certificate, a copy or the original commercial invoice, a copy or the original shipping documents, the copies or original documents of other transportation contracts and a survey report should be submitted according to the important clause. All these documents, with a statement of claim attached, are used to make a claim. Depending on the damage level, other documents may be needed.

In the particular average, insurance is calculated by the disadvantageous rate multiplied by the contract amount covered. However, if cargo is sold during the transportation, insurance is paid by deducting the sale from the contract amount. This is called salvage loss payment.

In the case of total loss, the total amount is paid. In constructive total loss, the insurant is paid based on abandonment. If the cost of saving the cargo is higher than the cargo's value, it is more reasonable to abandon the cargo. This behavior is called abandonment. In the case of abandonment, the insurant has to issue a notice of abandonment to the insurance company.

3-3-3 Claim for General Average

When all of the cargo encounters danger during transportation, the captain abandons some cargo in order to save the other cargoes to lower the loss. The loss caused by the abandoned cargoes is shared by the ship owner, all of the cargo's owners and those who acquired transportation fare. This is called general average. The York-Antwerp Rules was adopted in order to unify the way of calculating the general average. These rules were revised in 1974 and have been used until now.

If the loss of cargo is notified by the shipping company as general average, the importer should ask the judge to make arrangements for judgment. When either particular average or general average is decided, the insurant should submit the necessary documents required by the important clause to the insurance company for claim. If the importer did not lose cargo in the general average, the general average bond, valuation paper, commercial invoice, general average guarantee should be submitted to the shipping company. The general average bond is a promise made to share the loss in the general average. The valuation paper shows the price of the cargo when it has reached the destination; the CIF price is usually used. The general average guarantee is a promise made by the insurance company to share the loss in the general average. The insurant should request this document from the insurance company. The general average's settlement is done by a general average settling agent. This procedure usually takes a long time. The cargo's owner cannot receive the cargo from the shipping company unless the general average deposit is paid because the shipping company keeps the lien of the cargo.

3-3-4 Insurance Receiving

The insurance company gets a subrogation instead of paying the insurance. The subrogation entitles the insurance company the right to be the insured. The insurance company can acquire the right to make a claim within the range of the paid insurance. When the insurance is paid, the insured has to submit a letter of subrogation to the insurance company to transfer its subrogation.

4 Trade Claim

4-1 What Is Trade Claim

The conflicts caused by sales contract between the sellers and the buyers is called trade claim. This is a claim for a breach of contract caused by the seller or buyer. In law, the claim is the right to claim for immunity and is different from the one used in daily life.

Most claims of the exporters are about the importer's payment for the cargo, such as refusing or delaying to make a payment. If it is a L/C payment, most claims are about delaying to issue the L/C or discrepancy in the contract.

Most claims of the importers are about the quality or quantity of the import cargo, as well as the delivery date and receiving the cargo.

There are more claims in international trade than in domestic trade. The reason is that international sales contract starts when a breach of contract occurs. Moreover, sales contract are perceived differently in different countries.

Trade contracts are based on the promises to execute in the future. There is a time difference between the approval of the trade contract and fulfillment of the trade contract. This is called executory contract for sale of goods. It is possible that something cannot be expected at the time of agreement and the implementation of contract is also not definite. In international trade, after the contract is concluded, there may be changes in situation, not to mention misunderstandings that may lead to non-performance of the contract.

There is no international business practice or international law system for international trade. There are some international regulations, such as the uniform customs and practice for documentary credits and Incoterms. However, they are not practical in international trade.

International trade is based on contracts. In Asia, an oral contract is used and regarded as important in business practice from time to time. On the other hand, western countries prefer to write the documentary contract.

4-2 Claim Bringing and Problem Settlement

Usually, the way for the importer to make a claim to the exporter is written in the sales contract. After the importer receives the cargo, a claim can be made within certain days. It is necessary for the importer to attach a survey report in order to make a claim.

It is ideal for a claiming problem to be solved by negotiation.

This is called compromise. If negotiations cannot solve the problem, intercession, conciliation, arbitration and lawsuit can be used to solve it.

In intercession, a third party acts as an intercessor and tries to solve the problem. The intercessor can be the chamber of commerce and the consular. The intercessor gives advice instead of making judgments.

After listening to each party, the conciliator makes a proposal to solve the conflict. This is called conciliation. However, either party has no obligation to take the proposal. Whether the problem can be solved or not depends on each party's opinion about the proposal.

In arbitration, an arbitrator gives an arbitral award and solves the problem. The judgment by the arbitrator is enforceable to both parties. This is used the most to solve problems in international trade due to its efficiency. Another way is to make a lawsuit and solve the problem. The judgment is also enforceable to both parties, but the judgment itself differs from the court.

The final way to solve the problem is written in the sales contract. Usually, either arbitration or lawsuit is adopted.

4-3 Arbitration and Lawsuit

There are some differences between a lawsuit and arbitration. Arbitration usually takes fewer days than the lawsuit. Arbitration is just one time while a lawsuit can be several times. Usually, arbitration is cheaper than lawsuit. The lawsuit is open to the public while arbitration is closed. An advantage of arbitration is that it can protect the secret information of both parties or their contract. However, you cannot claim even if unjustified judgment might be made and you tend to have middle course arbitrations. The enforcement of lawsuit is limited its country while arbitration is enforceable among signatories.

4-4 Claim Handling Procedure

If the claim for immunity is approved either way, immunity can be remitted to the claimant through the bank. The compensation to the claim also can be in goods, such as additional goods to the exported goods or replacement of defective goods given to the importer for free. Allowance to the goods is also a way to compensate.

Questions

1 Explain the procedure of customs clearance and receiving imported cargo.
2 Briefly explain insurance claim.
3 Give a comparison on lawsuit and arbitration in terms of solutions for Trade claim. Discuss in class the advantages and disadvantages of each.

Main References

Michael Bridge, *the International Sale of Goods --- Law and Practice*, Oxford University Press, 1999

Alex L. Parks, *The Law and Practice of Marine Insurance and Average Vol. 1&2*, Cornell Maritime Press, 1987

Ronald A. Brand, *Fundamental of International Business Transaction*, Kluwer Law International, 2000

Zak Karamally, *Export Savvy*, International Business Press, 1998

Clive M. Schmitthoff & Paul Dobson, *Charlesworth's Business Law 15th ed.*, Sweet & Maxwell, 1991

Robert Crime, *Shipping Law 2nd ed.*, Sweet & Maxwell, 1991

John W. Hardwicke & Robert W Emerson, *Business Law*, Barron's Educational Series Inc., 1992

William C. Hillman, *Letters of Credit*, Butterworth Legal Publishers, 1987

Nigel Savage & Robert Bradgate, *Business Law*, Butterworth, 1987

Jim Sherlock, *Principles of International Physical Distribution*, Blackwell Publishers, 1994

Peter Sarcevic & Paul Volken, The international Sale of Goods Revised, Kluwer Law International, 2001

Carl A. Nelson, *Import Export*, McGraw-Hill, 1995

Edward G. Hinkelman, *International Payment*, World Trade Press, 2002

Karla C. Shippey, *International Contracts*, World Trade Press, 2003

Edward G. Hinkelman, *International Trade Documentation*, World Trade Press, 2001

Belay Seyoum, *Export-Import Theory, Practices and Procedures*, international Business Press, 2000

Gabriel Moens & Peter Gillies, *International Trade and Business*, Cabendish Pub., 2000

David M. Neipert, *A Tour of International Trade*, Prentice Hall, 2000

Larry A. Dimatteo, *The Law of International Business Transactions*, Thomson, 2002

Dornier, Ernest, Fender & Kouvelis, *Global Operations and Logistics*, John Wiley & Sons, 1998

Alan Branch, *Export Practice and Management*, Business Press, 2000

Albaum, Strandskov & Duerr, *International Marketing and Export Management*, Addison-Wesley, 1998

Nicholas Kouladis, *Principles of Law Relating to Overseas Trade*, Blackwell Pub., 1994

Main References 169

Andreas F. Lowenfeld, *International Private Trade*, Matthew & Bender, 1996
Pamela Sellman ed., *Law of International Trade*, Old Bailey Press, 2003
Pamela Sellman ed., 150 Leading Case *Law of International Trade*, Old Bailey Press, 2003
John S. Gordon, *Export/Import Letters of Credit and Payment Methods*, Global Training Center, 2002
Koji Tsubaki, *Fundamental Trade operations*, Japan Economy News Press, 2001
Tetsuji Kurusu, *Basic Trade operations 10th ed.*, Dobunkan, 2003
Satoshi Niihori, *Practical Trade Transaction*, Japan Economy News Press, 1998
Yasushi Fukuda & Kenji Yokoyama, *Trade Practice 5th ed.*, Seibido, 2003
Kenji Yokoyama, *Air Transport and Trade System*, Dobunkan, 2000

Index

【A】

Abandonment　161
Acceptance　48
Acceptance Advice　149
Acceptance Rate　149
Accepting Bank　112
Actual Carrier　139
Actual Delivery　37
Actual Total Loss　99
Ad Valorem Duties　154
Additional Charges　80
Advance Payment　54
Advance Sample　140
Advising Bank　111
Agent　4, 22
Air Cargo Agent　89, 139
Air Line Company　6
Air Waybill　89, 139
Air-NACCS　153
All Risks　26, 59, 100
Allowance　53, 165
Amendment　110
Amount　53
Applicant　111
Application for Irrevocable Letter of Credit　110
Application for Marine Insurance　102
Application for Space　80
Arbitral Award　164
Arbitration　28, 164
Arrival Notice　156
At Sight　147
ATA Carnet　137

【B】

B/L Crisis　86
Back to Back Credit　115
Bailee Clause　158
Bank Opinion　18
Bank Reference　18
Battle of Forms　29
Beneficiary　111
Berth Terms　81
Bid Bond　113
Bilateral Netting　130
Bill Bought　149
Bill of Lading　82
Blank Endorsement　84
Bonded/Hozei Exposition　134
Bonded/Hozei Factory　134
Bonded/Hozei Transportation　134
Bonded/Hozei Warehouse　134
Booking Note　80
Box Rate　79
Break Down Method　36
Bulk Breaking Agent　156
Bulk Cargo　133
Bunker Surcharge　80
Buyer's Sample　31
Buying Agent　4, 22
Buying Contract　127
Buying Contract Slip　128

【C】

C&F　42, 46
Calendar Month Delivery with Option　128
Call Option　129

Index   171

Capacity   18
Capital   18
Captain's Protest   160
Cargo Insurance   58
Carrier's Pack   138
Catalog   18, 31
Catch-All Restrictions   65
Certificate and List of Measurement and/or Weight   135, 142
Certificate of Insurance   142
Certificate of Origin   69, 142
Certificate of Pre-shipment Inspection   142
Certificate of Quality Inspection   69
Certificate of Quarantine   69
CFR   42
Chamber of Commerce and Industry   17
Character   19
Charter Party   74, 81, 85
Chartering Broker   81
CIF   42, 43
CIF + 10%   59
CIP   44
Claim Note   159
Claim Settling Agent   161
Clean B/L   85
Clean Credit   112
Combined Transport B/L   91
Combined Transport Document   88
Commercial Invoice   73, 107, 141
Commission   4, 22
Commodity Box Rate   79
Complaint   26
Compromise   164
Conciliation   164
Conditions   19

Confirmation   111
Confirmation of Order   49
Confirmed Credit   114
Confirming Bank   111
Congestion Surcharge   79
Consolidated Cargo   78, 139
Consolidator   78, 132
Constructive Total Loss   99, 161
Container Freight Station   138
Container Freight Station Cargo   74
Container Handling Charge   79
Container Load Plan   138
Container Yard Cargo   74
Contracting Carrier   139
Copyright   26
Correspondent Bank   19, 111
Cost Plus Method   36
Counter Offer   49
Counter Sample   32
Cover Note   103
CPT   43
CQD   82
Credit Information   19
Credit Inquiry   18
Credit Risk   104
Credit Standing   18
Cumulative Revolving Credit   114
Currency Option   129
Currency Surcharge   79
Customary Quick Dispatch   82
Customs   5
Customs Broker   6, 135

【D】
D/A   149

D/P   149
DAF   44
Damage Survey   159
DDP   45
DDU   45
Dead Freight   80
Debit Advice   148
Deferred Payment Credit   115
Definite Declaration   103
Delivery   60
Delivery Order   156
Delivery Record   156, 158
Demurrage   82, 157
DEQ   45
DES   44
DESCRIPTION   51
Design Right   27
Designated Bonded/Hozei Area   134
Destination Contract   37
Devanning Report   157
Direct Cargo   38, 138
Directory   17
Discrepancy   117, 147
Dispatch Money   82, 157
Distributor   4, 22
Divided Liability System   93
Dock Receipt   85, 138
Document of Title   82
Documentary Bill of Exchange   141
Documentary Clean Credit   112
Documentary Collection   57
Documentary Letter of Credit   55
Documents against Acceptance   57
Documents against Payment   57
Double Guarantee   86

Drawee   112
Duplicate Sample   32

【E】
E. & O. E.   33
Emergency Risk   104
Entire Agreement   28
Equipment Receipt   137
Exchange Marry   129
EXF   46
Export Declaration   135
Export License   64
Export Permit   135
Exporter   4
EXW   40, 46

【F】
Factor   125
Factoring   125
FAQ   32
FAS   40
FCA   42
FI   81
Final Claim   159
FIO   81
Firm Offer   49
Fixture Note   81
FO   81
FOB   41, 46
FOB Attachment Clause   101
Force Majeure   27
Foreign Access Zone   134
Foreign Exchange Risk   126
Forfeiting   111, 114
Form A   69

Index   173

Forward Exchange Contract   127
Forwarder   6, 72, 133
Forwarder's B/L   86
Foul B/L   85
FPA   50, 99
Free From Particular Average   99
Free In   81
Free In and Out   81
Free Out   81
Freight All Kinds Box Rate   79
Freight Ton   79
Full Container Load Cargo   74
Full Insurance   95
Fumigation Certificate   69

【G】

G.A. Bond   162
G.A. Deposit   162
G.A. Guarantee   162
Gate Clerk   138
General Average   99, 160
General Credit   114
General Terms and Conditions   21
GMQ   32

【H】

Hague Rules   84
Hague Visby Rules   84
Hatch Survey   159
House Air Waybill   90, 139

【I】

ICC (A) (B) (C)   59, 101
Immediate Shipment   60
Import Declaration   153

Import Permit   154
Import Quota   67
Important Clause   158
Importer   4
Incoterms   28, 39
Independence Principle   115
Inspection Certificate   70, 142
Institute of London Underwriters   96
Insurable Interest   95
Insurable Value   95
Insurance Agent   102
Insurance Broker   102
Insurance Certificate   103
Insurance Company   5
Insurance Policy   96, 142
Insurance Premium   96
Insured Amount   95
Insurer   95
Integrated Bonded/Hozei Area   134
Intercession   164
International Air Transport Association   88
International Chamber of Commerce   39
International Commercial Terms   39
International Marketing   14
International Trade Fair   17, 134
Inter-office Transaction   4
Irrevocable Credit   113
Irrevocable Letter of Credit   117
Issuing Bank   111

【J】

Japan External Trade Organization   17
JETRO   17

【K】
Knockout Forward　128

【L】
L/G Negotiation　147
Landed Quantity Terms　23
Latent Defect　26
Lawsuit　164
Laydays Statement　157
Leads and Lags　130
Less Than Container Load Cargo　74
Letter of Credit　25, 109
Letter of Guarantee　135, 151
Letter of Intent　28
Letter of Subrogation　162
Lien　162
Liner Terms　81
Loan Form Payment　160
Long Ton　53

【M】
Mail Transfer　55
Major Import Cargo Tariff Agreement　102
Margin　4, 22
Master Air Waybill　90, 139
Mate's Receipt　85
Maximum Quantity Acceptable　25
Mercantile Credit Agency　20
Metric Ton　53
Middle Rate　145
Minimum Quantity Acceptable　25
Minutes　51
More or Less Clause　53
Multilateral Netting　130
Multi-modal Transport　78
Multi-Modal Transport Documents　85

【N】
N.V.D.　90
Negotiating Bank　111
Negotiation　54, 111, 124
Netting　130
Network Liability System　93
Non-Cumulative Revolving Credit　114
Non-Vessel Operating Common Carrier　78
Notice of Abandonment　161
Notice of Damage　158
Notice of Readiness　157
Notifying Bank　111
NVOCC　78

【O】
Offer　48
Offer Subject to Confirmation　49
Offer Subject to Prior Sale　49
On Board Notation　85, 138
Open Account　55, 145
Open Policy　103
Opening Bank　111
Option Premium　129
Order　49
Order B/L　84
Original Sample　32
Over Insurance　95

【P】
Packing List　73, 142
Pamphlet　31
Partial Loss　98
Partial Shipment　25

Index   175

Particular Average   98
Patent Defect   26
Patent Right   26
Paying Bank   112, 148
Payment   54
Performance Bond   114
Power of Attorney   51
Preferential Duties   155
Preliminary Claim   158
Pre-Shipment Inspection   69
Price   53
Price List   17, 33
Principal   4
Principal-to-Principal Basis   22
Product Liability   5, 106
Proforma Invoice   33, 50, 153
Provisional Policy   103
Purchase Contract   50
Purchase Note   50
Put Option   129

【Q】
Quality   52
Quantity   53
Quotaions   33

【R】
Range Forward   128
Received B/L   85
Rejecting Letter   160
Release Order   158
Replacement   165
Reshipment   135
Revised American Foreign Trade Definitions   39

Revocable Credit   113
Revolving Credit   114
Running Laydays   82

【S】
Sale by Brand or Trade Mark   33
Sale by Description   32
Sale by Grade   32
Sale by Sample   31
Sale by Specifications   32
Sale by Standard   32
Sale Note   51
Sales Agent   21
Sales Contract   50
Salvage Loss Settlement   161
Sample   18, 32
Sea Waybill   87
Sea-NACCS   135, 153
Selling Contract   127
Selling Contract Slip   128
Shipment   60
Shipment Contract   37
Shipped B/L   84
Shipped Quantity Terms   23
Shipper's Interest   104
Shipper's Pack   138
Shipping Advice   139
Shipping Company   6
Shipping Documents   55, 120, 141
Shipping Instructions   73
Shipping Marks   133
Shipping Sample   140
Shipping Schedule   80
Shipping Space   80
Short Form B/L   85

Short Ton   53
Similar Sample   31
Single Guarantee   86
Special Credit   114
Special Endorsement   84
Specific Duties   154
Specific Terms and Conditions   21, 47
Spot Exchange Contract   127
Stale Documents   146
Stand-by Credit   113
Statement of Claim   161
Stevedore   157
Storage Charge   80
Straight B/L   84
Strict Compliance Principle   116
subject to export license   66
subject to import license   68
Subject-matter Insured   95
Subrogation   162
Supplier's Credit   58, 126
Surcharge   80
Surrendered B/L   87
Survey Report   26, 159
Surveyor   159
Sworn Measurer   134
Symbolic Delivery   37

[T]
Tariff Quota System   155
Telegraphic Transfer   55
Telegraphic Transfer Buying Rate   145
Telegraphic Transfer Selling Rate   145
Terminal Handling Charge   80
The Insured   95
The Uniform Customs and Practice for Documentary Credits   117
Through B/L   85
To Order of Shipper   84
Total Loss   99, 161
Trade Finance   7, 125
Trade Insurance   104
Trade Reference   20
Trade Terms   36
Trademark Right   26
Transit Clause   100
Transport Documents   142
Transshipment   25
Triplicate Sample   32
Trust Receipt   149, 156

[U]
Unconfirmed Credit   114
Under Insurance   95
Uniform Liability System   91
Unit Price   53
USQ   32
Utility Model Right   26

[V]
Valuation Paper   162
Vanning   136
Vessel Operating Common Carrier   78
VOCC   78

[W]
WA   59, 100
War & S.R.C.C. Risks   24
Warranty   27
Wassenaar Arrangement   64
Weather Working Days   80

With Average *99*	**【Y】**
With Recourse *124*	Yen Adjustment Surcharge *80*
Without Recourse *124*	York-Antwerp Rules *163*
WWD *82*	

■著者紹介

横山　研治（よこやま　けんじ）

立命館アジア太平洋大学経営管理研究科教授。博士（経営学）。1955年福岡県生まれ。早稲田大学政経学部卒。著書に『航空運送における定型取引条件の実証的研究』（単著、比較文化研究所刊、1991、貿易奨励会奨励賞受賞）、『我国で使用されるトレードタームズの動向調査』（共著、日本大学産業経営研究所刊、1997、貿易奨励会奨励賞受賞）、『航空運送と貿易システム』（単著、同文舘、2000、日本貿易学会奨励賞受賞）、『韓国の国際通商法』（共著、大学教育出版、2002）などがある。

International Trade Operations

2006年10月10日　初版第1刷発行

■著　者──横山研治
■発行者──佐藤　守
■発行所──株式会社 大学教育出版
　　　　　〒700-0953　岡山市西市855-4
　　　　　電話 (086) 244-1268㈹　FAX (086) 246-0294
■印刷製本──モリモト印刷㈱
■装　丁──ティーボーンデザイン事務所

Ⓒ Kenji YOKOYAMA 2006, Printed in Japan
検印省略　落丁・乱丁本はお取り替えいたします。
無断で本書の一部または全部を複写・複製することは禁じられています。

ISBN4-88730-716-0